AF255185

GRAMMAR

MADE EASY

Intermediate

by Mat Wilton

Publisher information and year

ISBN-13: 978-0-6453950-2-0

SUBJECT PRONOUN "I"

09

PRONOUN "SHE"

26

VERB FAMILY TREE

37

PRESENT TENSE: VERBS

53

PRONOUN PYRAMID

57

"The zebras, a breed of black horses with white stripes, are recognised individually through the placement of their lines. They're barcoded! Words can be similarly coded, by association with a sign, to learn their separate roles within a bunch of text. The endless combination of words, the constant changing outline of the textual herd, can now be traced and understood through pattern recognition. (And, as human beings, we are innately very good at it.) Hence, the zebra logo."

by Mat Wilton

How PICTURES work

Grammar is not a lot of writing. Grammar is about thinking how a sentence works, making connections and having learning conversations. A sentence then, is an analytical problem answerable by Grammar. A sentence is a finished jigsaw, without the delineation of individual pieces. I'm just putting those lines back in: Grammar has become a visual medium and its rules are visually available.

Great writing is created through the knowledge and manipulation of phrases: you can develop wonderful style, if you know the grammar.

This second book continues with the out-of-the-square approach to understanding traditional grammar through the uniqueness of Pictorial Grammar Theory: the motions of pictorially describing a sentence. The images are elegant in both their simplicity and economy. Complexities are easily grasped and then reinforced each time an image is drawn, transforming sentences into a cohesive structure, aesthetically pleasing. Presentation continues in manageable steps aimed at mastering a grammatical concept.

Subject Pronouns are introduced and then fashioned into a Pronoun Pyramid. The pyramid is aligned to the conjugation of verbs: the quintessential aspect of English in the matching of a main character (subject) to the correct form of the verb. Verbs are also seen as Time Travellers, creating tenses in the present, past and future. The Picture for the verb becomes more detailed, with hands of time making a clear signpost for the tenses: just building on the knowledge already established. The learner will be able to appreciate how verbs can be used to construct phrases.

Pictorial Grammar Theory:
Simple stories are coupled with semiotic* imagery that underlies a brand-new, innovative, and divergent pedagogy on the teaching and learning of grammar. Scarcely a word is written, as students overlay powerfully understood symbols/images upon the text: any text. The image is a synthesis of the word's function within a sentence. Sentences are transformed into a pleasing aesthetic of connected images.

*Semiotics: based on "semiosis," the relationship between a sign, an object, and a meaning.

YOU CAN FIND MORE EXERCISES AND RESOURCES AT

www.profstripes.com

PICTURE 11: Subject Pronoun "I"

> **The first person singular form is "I".**

As we learnt in Book 1, nouns can be framed in a box, have a shadow, and as a main character have a spotlight. Once we know the noun, we can substitute with a subject pronoun. (Repeating the noun over and over would make our writing clumsy.)

Subject pronouns have:
- a short shadow as nothing will ride on it
- do not have determiners or adjectives
- and they refer back to a noun, already known to us.

When a writer uses "I", they are writing about themselves. This is called writing in the first person and the first person is pretty important, so they get an important hat.

Subject Pronoun "I" Examples:

In the examples below, "I" is referring back to the character already known to us.

In the first example "I" is referring back to "Peter", already known to us, and in the second example "I" is referring back to "Rebecca", already known to us. Note that the two examples are separate stories.

Just using the noun.

Substituting the pronoun:

Just using the noun.

Rebecca is my name. Rebecca came from Italy.

Substituting the pronoun:

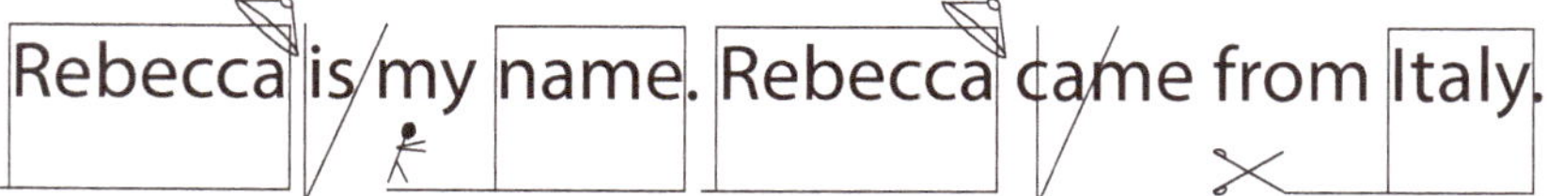

Subject Pronoun "I" Exercise

Box the nouns, grow the shadow, stopping under the determiner.
Go over the subject pronouns with the correct Picture. Include the spotlight.
The remaining word will be the verb.

I did the shopping.

I broke my pencil.

I chased the dog.

I found the kitten.

I painted my room.

I hit the ball.

Story 1:

Tim is the writer of these sentences. Tim is also the main character. He is writing in the first person. Replace this main character with the subject pronoun "I". Include the spotlight. Do all of the images.

On a wonderful spring morning Tim rose from a comfy bed.

Tim heard the sound of the birds in the nearby trees.

From the kitchen Tim heard the grownups. Tim ran

down the stairs and headed for the breakfast table.

Tim was extremely hungry.

Subject Pronoun "I" Answers

Box the nouns, grow the shadow, stopping under the determiner.
Go over the subject pronouns with the correct Picture. Include the spotlight.
The remaining word will be the verb.

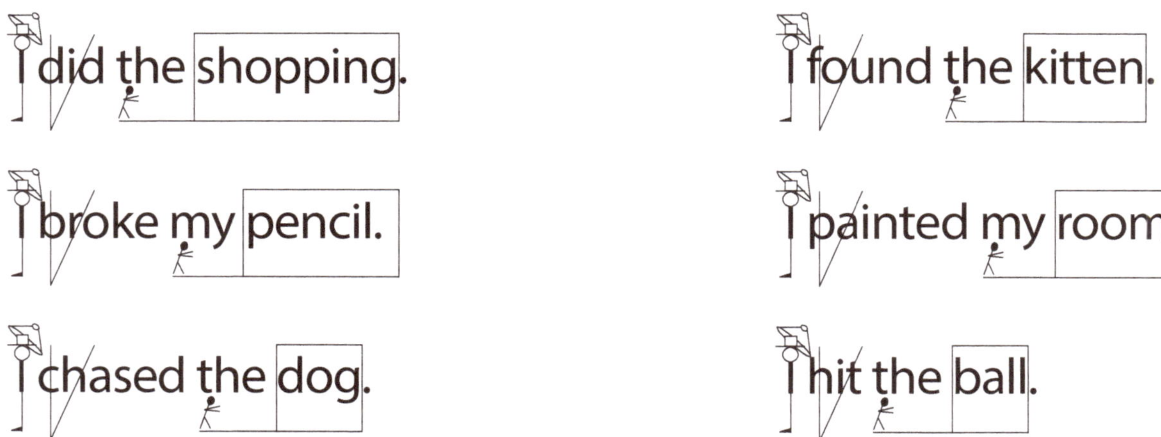

I did the shopping.   I found the kitten.

I broke my pencil.   I painted my room.

I chased the dog.   I hit the ball.

Story 1:

Tim is the writer of these sentences. Tim is also the main character. He is writing in the first person. Replace this main character with the subject pronoun "I". Include the spotlight. Do all of the images.

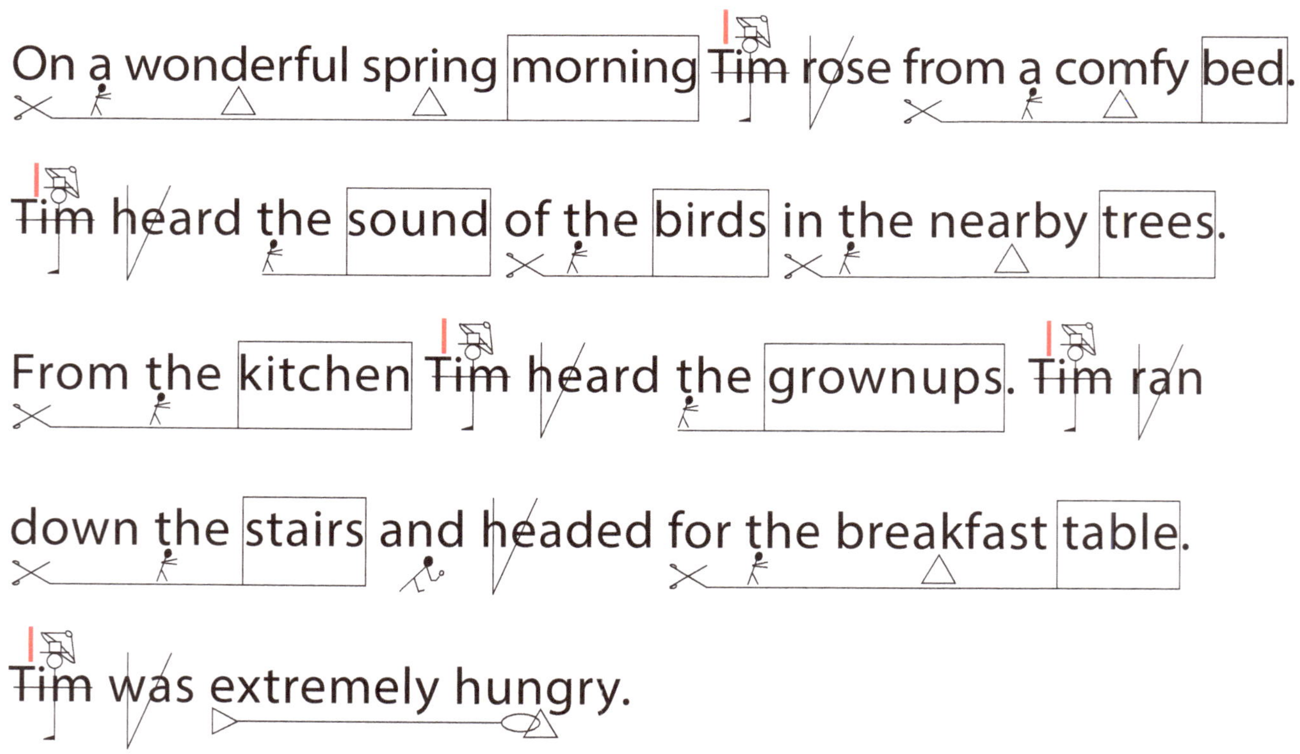

On a wonderful spring morning Tim rose from a comfy bed.

Tim heard the sound of the birds in the nearby trees.

From the kitchen Tim heard the grownups. Tim ran

down the stairs and headed for the breakfast table.

Tim was extremely hungry.

PICTURE 12: Subject Pronoun "We"

When a writer uses "we", they are still writing about themselves, and their group of friends. This style of writing is still called writing in the first person.

"We" is the plural form of the first person.

> " The first person plural form is "we".

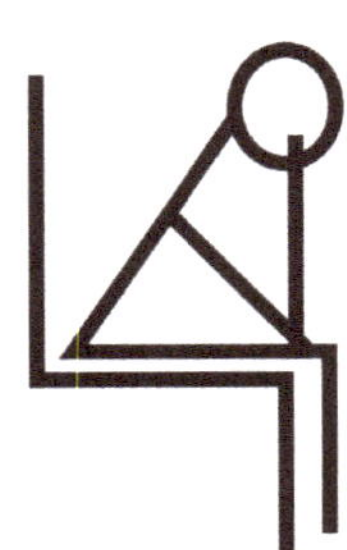

Subject Pronoun "We" Examples:

The example has three main characters.

Sally, Toni and Peter are our names.

In the winter Sally, Toni and Peter played netball.

Sally, Toni and Peter surfed in the summer.

Substituting the main character with the pronoun "we".

Sally, Toni and Peter are our names.

In the winter we played netball.

We surfed in the summer.

Subject Pronoun "We" Exercise

The writer has two main characters, Sonya and Stevie. This writer is writing in the first person. Replace these main characters with the subject pronoun "we". Include the spotlight and other related Pictures.

Story 1: A Diary Entry

Sonya and Stevie walked along a popular trail above the cliffs. Sonya and Stevie watched the crashing of the waves and Sonya and Stevie admired the ocean's tremendous force. On a weathered bench Sonya and Stevie shared a sandwich.

The writer has two main characters, Sonya and Stevie. This writer is writing in the first person. Replace these main characters with the subject pronoun "we". Include the spotlight and other related Pictures.

Story 1: A Diary Entry

We Sonya and Stevie walked along a popular trail above the cliffs. We Sonya and Stevie watched the crashing of the waves and we Sonya and Stevie admired the ocean's tremendous force. On a weathered bench we Sonya and Stevie shared a sandwich.

PICTURE 13: Subject Pronoun "You"
Singular Form

When a writer uses "you", they are writing about the closest person to them, someone in the room they could reach out and touch. The writer is next to this person. This sort of writing is called "writing in the second person".

The picture is based on the letter "Y" for you.

> " The second person singular form is "you". "

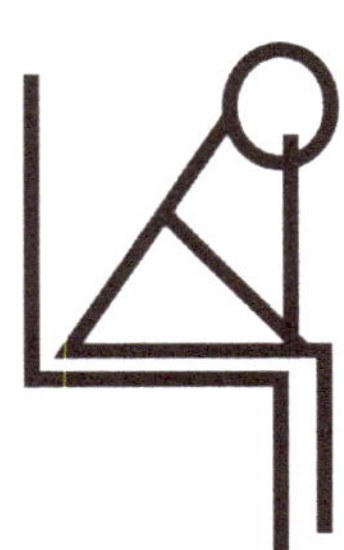

Subject Pronoun "You" Examples

The writer reminding someone of their adventure.

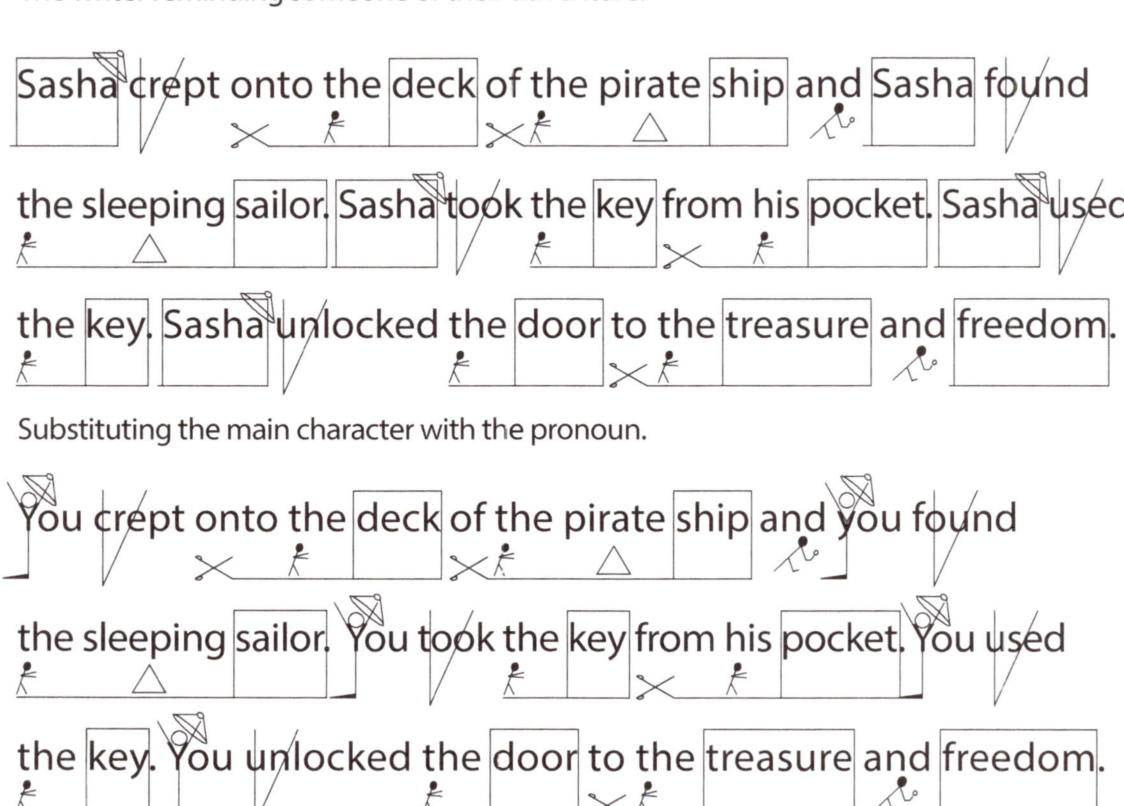

Sasha crept onto the deck of the pirate ship and Sasha found the sleeping sailor. Sasha took the key from his pocket. Sasha used the key. Sasha unlocked the door to the treasure and freedom.

Substituting the main character with the pronoun.

You crept onto the deck of the pirate ship and you found the sleeping sailor. You took the key from his pocket. You used the key. You unlocked the door to the treasure and freedom.

Subject Pronoun "You" Exercise

Writing in the second person, "you" is the only subject pronoun for both a single or more than one main character (see also Picture 14). In this exercise they are all single. Include the spotlight and other related Pictures.

Sentences:

You sharpened the pencil.

You made a cup of hot chocolate.

You took money from the machine.

Be the writer, reminding a close friend, Laura, of their adventure. Replace the noun Laura with the subject pronoun "you". Include the spotlight and other related Pictures. This becomes writing in the second person. Draw all of the Pictures.

Story 1:

Laura seemed jumpy on that morning. The flying insects were annoying. Laura tried breakfast, Laura tried a journal entry but Laura finally left the campsite and headed over the walls of the lost city. Laura found the rope and descended into another time.

Subject Pronoun "You" Answers

Writing in the second person, "you" is the only subject pronoun for both a single or more than one main character (see also Picture 14). In this exercise they are all single. Include the spotlight and other related Pictures.

Sentences:

You sharpened the pencil.

You made a cup of hot chocolate.

You took money from the machine.

Be the writer, reminding a close friend, Laura, of their adventure. Replace the noun Laura with the subject pronoun "you". Include the spotlight and other related Pictures. This becomes writing in the second person.

Story 1:

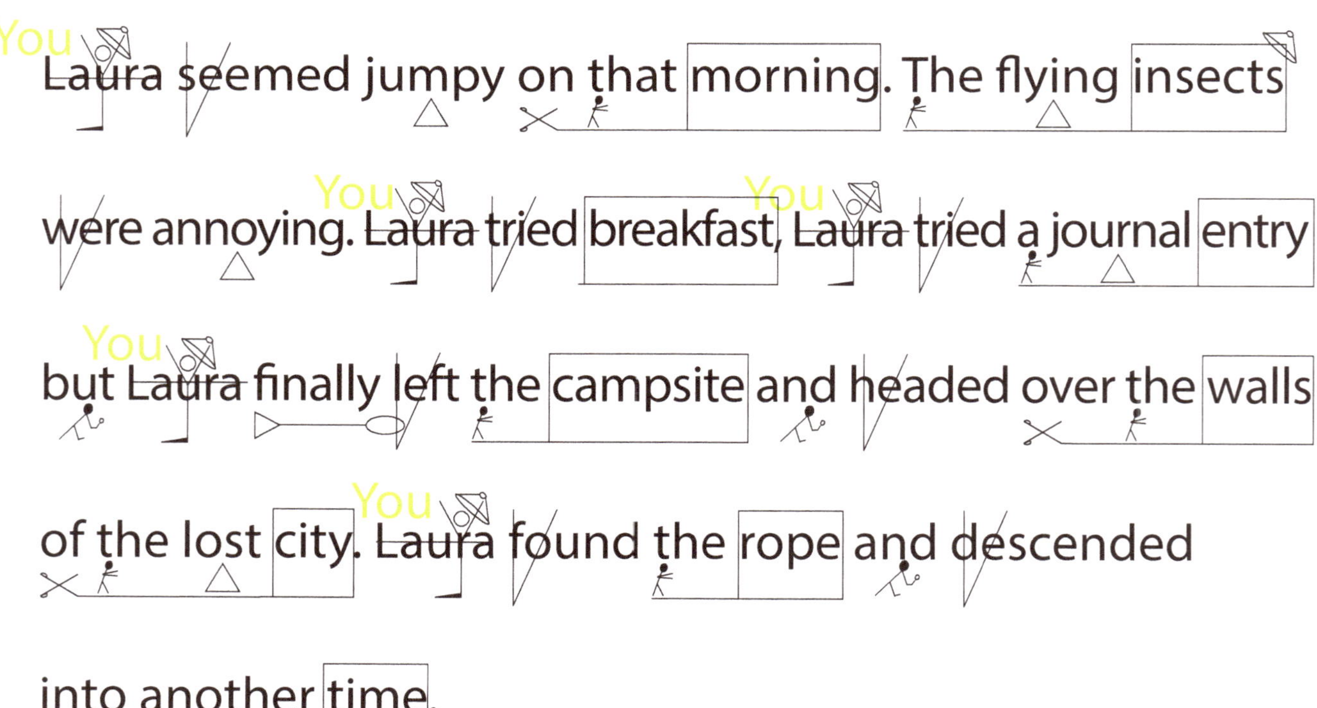

You Laura seemed jumpy on that morning. The flying insects were annoying. You Laura tried breakfast, You Laura tried a journal entry but You Laura finally left the campsite and headed over the walls of the lost city. You Laura found the rope and descended into another time.

PICTURE 14: Subject Pronoun "You"
Plural Form

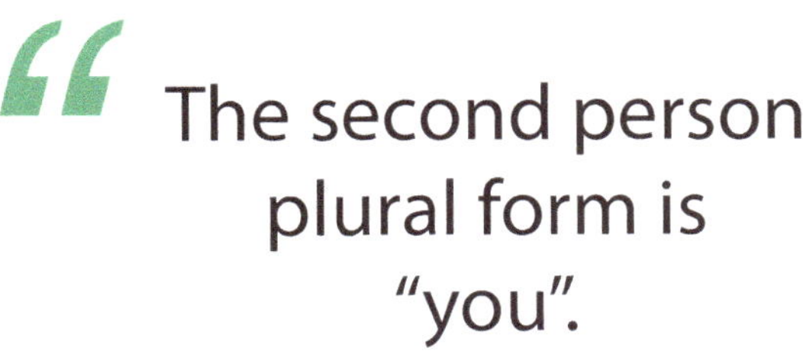

When a writer uses "you", they are also writing about the closest people to them, a team in the room they could reach out and touch. The writer is next to this group. "You" can be a plural pronoun, when writing in the second person.

" The second person plural form is "you".

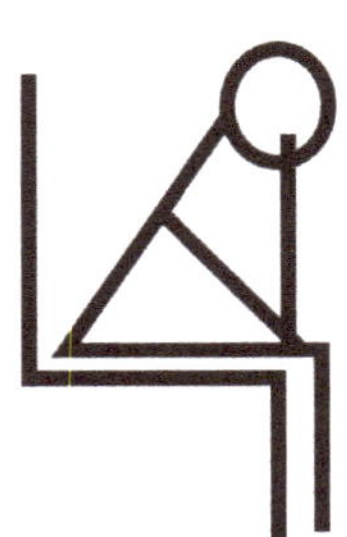

Subject Pronoun "You" Examples

The writer addressing a team.

Chloe, Tahlia and Naisha played beautifully in the first half.

In the second half the whole team lifted. The group became

dynamic. Alexandra and Elyse provided a strong defence.

Substituting the main character group with the pronoun.

You played beautifully in the first half.

In the second half you lifted. You became

dynamic. You provided a strong defence.

Subject Pronoun "You" Exercise

Writing in the second person, "you" is the only subject pronoun for both a single or more than one main character. Decide if the Picture for the pronoun should have one (Picture 13), or plural (Picture 14) heads. Include the spotlight and other related Pictures

Sentences:

You defeated the other team.

You were the best class.

You shot the first goal.

Be the writer, addressing a whole team. Replace the main character noun phrases with the subject pronoun "you". Include the spotlight and other related Pictures.

Story 1:

In the first quarter Isabel and Ava used the ball creatively.

Zara, Joanna and Annie dominated fiercely around the goals.

At the end of the third quarter the whole team looked

unstoppable. Arlo and Gemma were fresh substitutes

who boosted the defence.

Subject Pronoun "You" Answers

Writing in the second person, "you" is the only subject pronoun for both a single or more than one main character. Decide if the Picture for the pronoun should have one (Picture 13), or plural (Picture 14) heads. Include the spotlight and other related Pictures

Sentences:

You defeated the other team.

You were the best class.

You shot the first goal.

Be the writer, addressing a whole team. Replace the main character noun phrases with the subject pronoun "you". Include the spotlight and other related Pictures.

Story 1:

In the first quarter Isabel and Ava used the ball creatively.

Zara, Joanna and Annie dominated fiercely around the goals.

At the end of the third quarter the whole team looked

unstoppable. Arlo and Gemma were fresh substitutes

who boosted the defence.

PICTURE 15: Subject Pronoun "He"
Singular Form

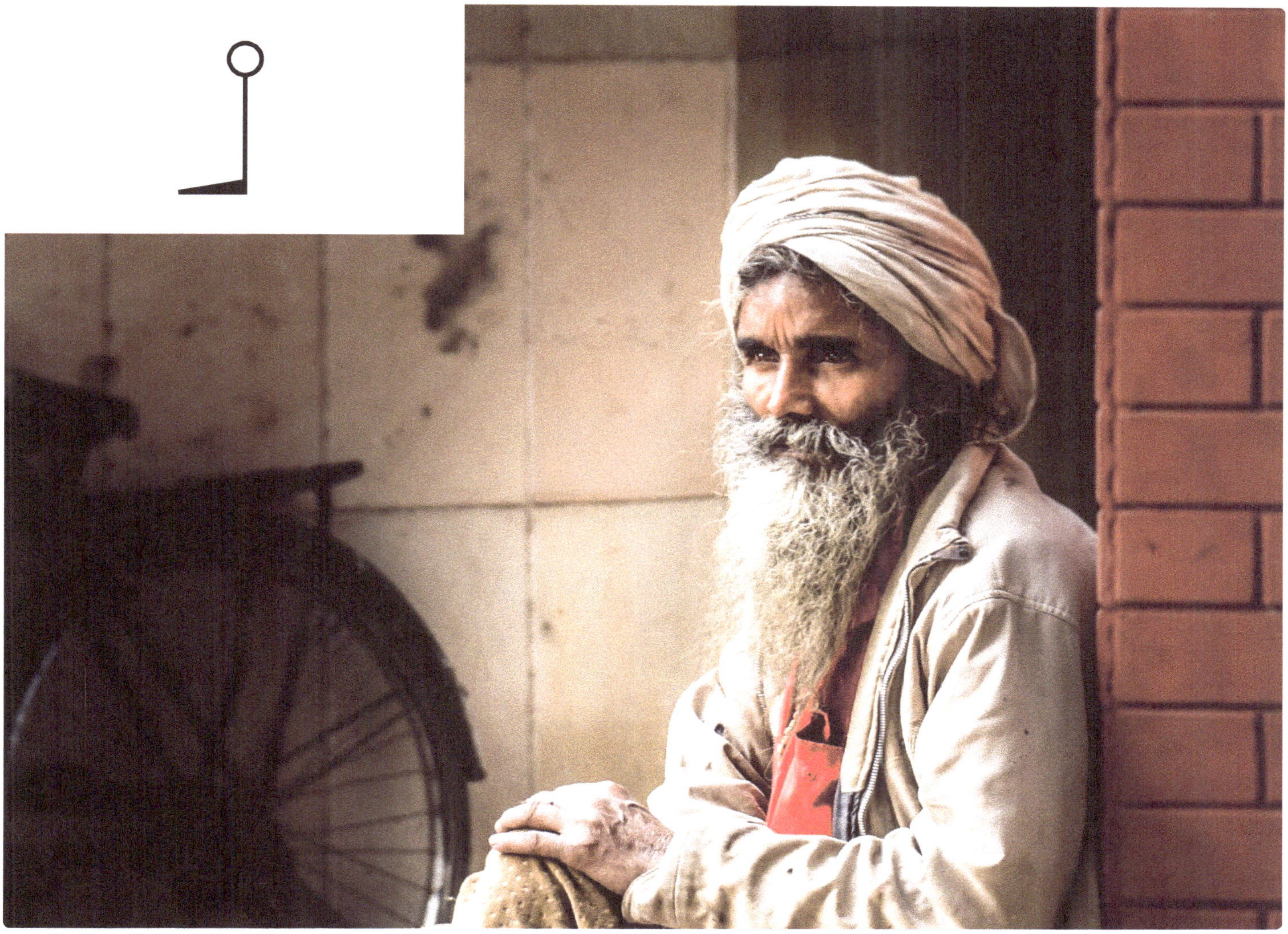

> "He" is third person singular.

When a writer uses "He", "She" or "It" they are writing about main characters who are really not known to them at all. The writer has no personal connection. In a room, these characters would be very far away from the writer, they would be the third person in the room (i.e. the writer, you and now this third person). This sort of writing is called writing in the third person. Remember that pronouns refer back to a noun already known to us, so using a name (a noun) is already writing in the third person. Most of the pieces we read, are written in the third person.

PICTURE 16: Subject Pronoun "She"
Singular Form

Think of a pronoun as a stunt person in a movie, being used instead of the real actor.

"She" is third person singular.

PICTURE 17: Subject Pronoun "It"
Singular Form

"It" is third person singular.

The subject pronoun "it" can be used when the gender of the subject is not specified or not a person.

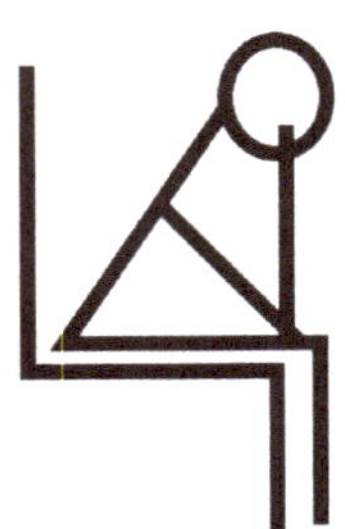

"He", "She", & "It" Examples

Here are three example sentences of writing in the third person

Mary skied furiously down the icy slope. Mary fell spectacularly into a deep crevasse.

With his new board Will leapt into the surging ocean. Will disappeared under a massive wave.

The brilliant kite zigzagged in the playful wind. The kite crashed into overhead powerlines.

Substituting the main character with the pronoun.

Mary skied furiously down the icy slope. She fell spectacularly into a deep crevasse.

With his new board Will leapt into the surging ocean. He disappeared under a massive wave.

The brilliant kite zigzagged in the playful wind. It crashed into overhead powerlines.

"He", "She", & "It" Exercise 1

The sentences are in pairs. Draw the spotlight in the first sentence and the other Pictures. In the second sentence, substitute the main character (subject) with the correct third person subject pronoun ("He", "She", or "It"). Include the other Pictures.

The clock was too old.   never showed the correct time.

Tim won the race. Across the finish line   shot like an arrow.

Amanda was a wonderful gardener.   loved the outdoors.

Replace the main character noun phrases with the correct subject pronoun. Think of the pronoun as a stunt double, doing all the dangerous action shots. This is writing in the third person. Include the spotlight and other related Pictures.

Story 1:

Matt was on a risky mission. Matt dodged the bullet and

Matt crawled to the doorway. Sukie was calm. Sukie

shattered the light with a single shot. In the darkness Matt

found the open window. Matt jumped. Sukie edged

near the same window. Sukie jumped.

"He", "She", & "It" Answers 1

The sentences are in pairs. Draw the spotlight in the first sentence and the other Pictures. In the second sentence, substitute the main character (subject) with the correct third person subject pronoun ("He", "She", or "It"). Include the other Pictures.

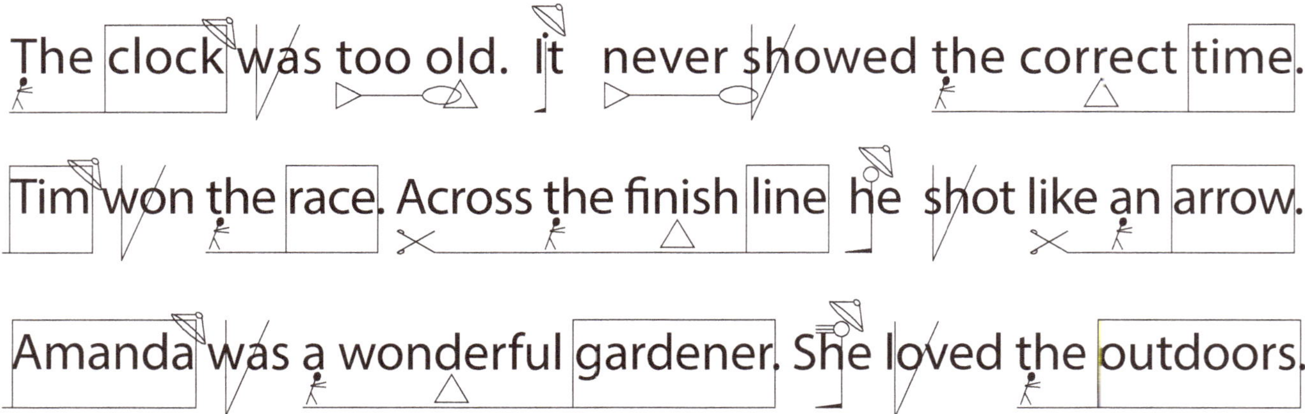

Replace the main character noun phrases with the correct subject pronoun. Think of the pronoun as a stunt double, doing all the dangerous action shots. This is writing in the third person. Include the spotlight and other related Pictures.

Story 1:

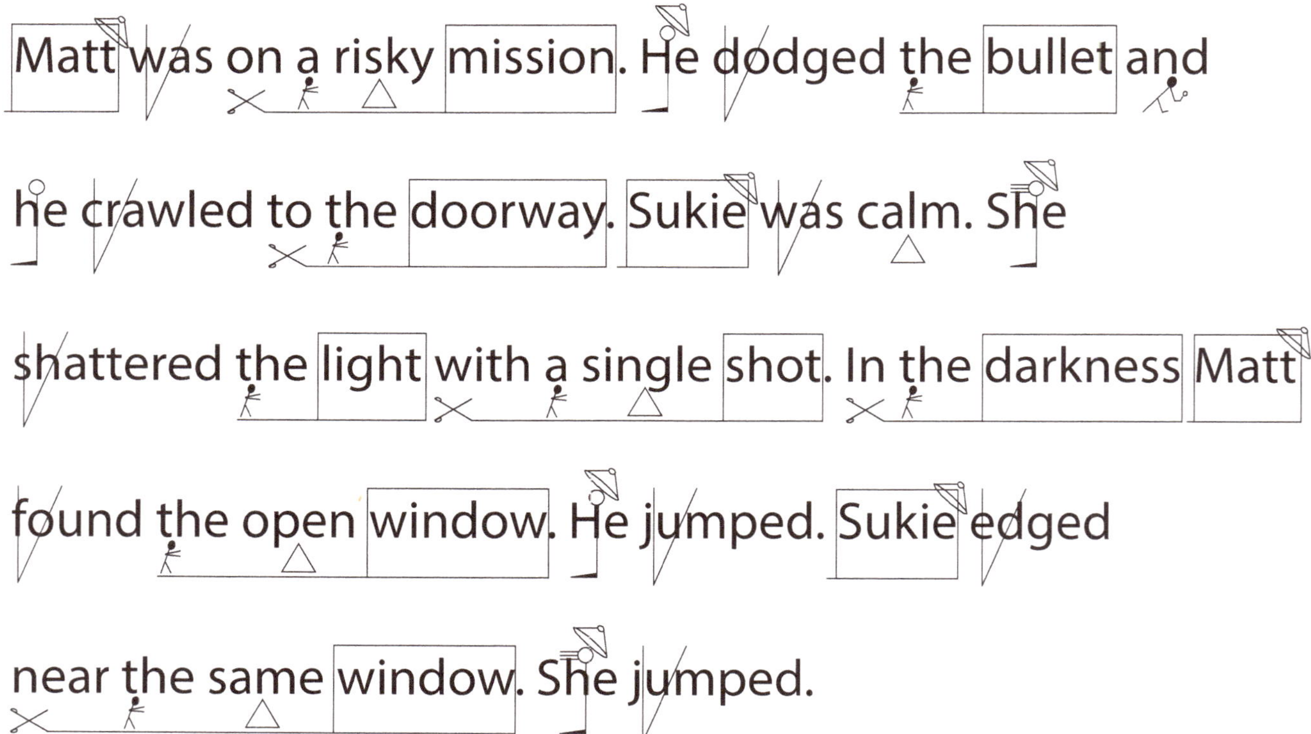

"He", "She", & "It" Exercise 2

The story has a number of main characters. In this exercise draw in the spotlight and the other pictures, then draw a line to show how the pronoun refers back to the noun we already know.
For example: noun   pronoun

Story 2:

Mark and Sky were in the garden. He tracked an ant. It

lugged a small seed. She watched a bird. It pecked steadily

in the bed of dry leaves. Peg sat on a rug. She had a cool hat.

It tied under the chin. Mark pointed at the ant. It was

really big.

◼ "He", "She", & "It" Answers 2

The story has a number of main characters. In this exercise draw in the spotlight and the other pictures, then draw a line to show how the pronoun refers back to the noun we already know. For example: noun   pronoun

Story 2:

Mark and Sky were in the garden. He tracked an ant. It lugged a small seed. She watched a bird. It pecked steadily in the bed of dry leaves. Peg sat on a rug. She had a cool hat. It tied under the chin. Mark pointed at the ant. It was really big.

PICTURE 18: Subject Pronoun "They"
Plural Form

> **"They" is third person plural.**

When "He", "She", or "It" just aren't enough! When the main character is more than one and still no personal connection to the writer. Using "They" refers back to nouns already known to us. Most pieces we read are written in the third person.

Note: As a non-binary or non-gendered pronoun, the subject pronoun "they" can be both plural and singular. See appendix page 95 for more details.

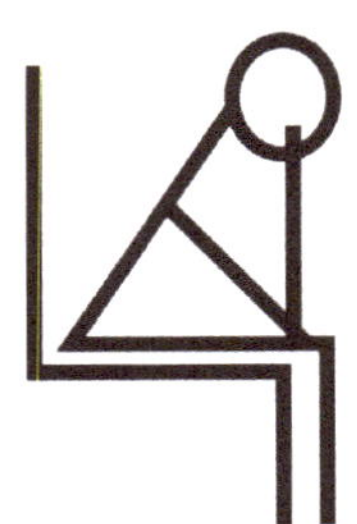# "They" Examples

Three example sentences of writing in the third person plural.

Arnie, Angie and Adam rode bikes across the barren desert.

Arnie, Angie and Adam desperately needed shelter from a sandstorm.

Substituting the main character with the pronoun.

Arnie, Angie and Adam rode bikes across the barren desert.

They desperately needed shelter from a sandstorm.

The witch's bell, book and candle escaped detection.

The bell, book and candle remained under the ancient floorboards.

Substituting the main character with the pronoun.

The witch's bell, book and candle escaped detection.

They remained under the ancient floorboards.

Into the pelting rain the migrating birds flew. The migrating birds

found protection in the trees of a nearby forest.

Substituting the main character with the pronoun.

Into the pelting rain the migrating birds flew. They

found protection in the trees of a nearby forest.

Subject Pronoun "They" Exercise

These sentences are in pairs. In the first sentence draw in the spotlight and the other Pictures. In the second sentence, substitute the main character (subject) with the correct third person subject pronoun. Draw all of the Pictures.

Sentences

Jesse and Jonas were old dogs.   often slept for the whole day.

The waves battered the coastline.   were a true force of nature.

The scientists loved the laboratory.   conducted vital research.

Replace the main character noun phrases with the correct subject pronoun. Include the spotlight and other related Pictures. Then draw a line to show how the pronoun refers back to the noun we already know. For example: noun   pronoun

Story 1:

The swings and slides in the park were new. They

clearly attracted Mark and Mia. He liked the swings. She

liked the exciting slides. The day was kind. It was

overcast with a pleasantly cool breeze. Friends

soon arrived. They wore sunscreen. It smelt of coconuts.

Subject Pronoun "They" Answers

These sentences are in pairs. In the first sentence draw in the spotlight and the other Pictures. In the second sentence, substitute the main character (subject) with the correct third person subject pronoun.

Sentences

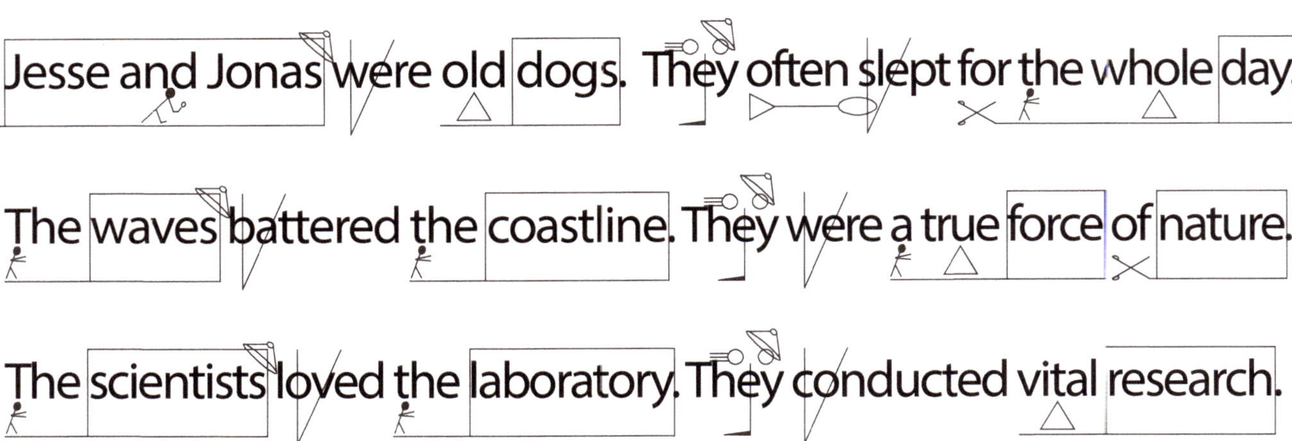

Jesse and Jonas were old dogs. They often slept for the whole day.

The waves battered the coastline. They were a true force of nature.

The scientists loved the laboratory. They conducted vital research.

Replace the main character noun phrases with the correct subject pronoun. Include the spotlight and other related Pictures. Then draw a line to show how the pronoun refers back to the noun we already know. For example: noun   pronoun

Story 1:

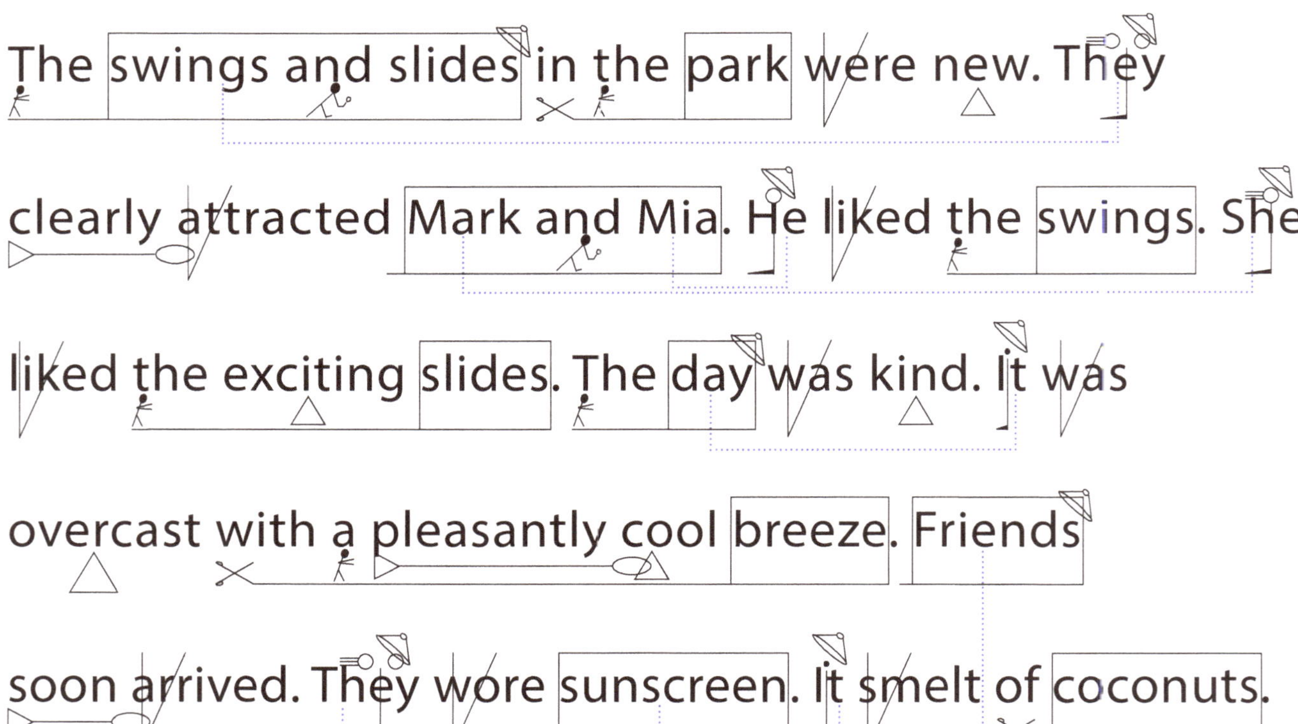

The swings and slides in the park were new. They

clearly attracted Mark and Mia. He liked the swings. She

liked the exciting slides. The day was kind. It was

overcast with a pleasantly cool breeze. Friends

soon arrived. They wore sunscreen. It smelt of coconuts.

PICTURE 19: The Verb Family Tree

> **Verbs, with their arrows, can point to the past, present and future.**

The verb, just like a family tree, has many members in its family. These family members or structures are all derived from the infinitive of the verb.

Essentially, the verb marks many places in time. Altogether a verb can be formed into 12 places in time. These are called tenses:
- some in the past
- some in the present
- and some in the future.

This excludes
- the infinitive of the verb as it is timeless
- and the participles used to construct tenses.

The Verb Family Tree

There are 3 time zones created from the infinitive of the verb. These are the (simple) tenses: past, present, and future (see appendix 1).

Timeless

∞

The Infinitive of the Verb

Past

Present

Future

Simple Past

Simple Present

Simple Future

Participles

Past Participle

Present Participle

(will) (have) Future Perfect

(will) (be) Future Progressive

Past Perfect

Present Perfect

(will) (have) (been) Future Perfect Progressive

Past Progressive

Present Progressive

(been) Past Perfect Progressive

(been) Present Perfect Progressive

> " Beginning with the infinitive, there are 15 formations of the verb which will be covered in this series. "

PICTURE 19a: The Infinitive of the Verb

The verb is a form class word*, because it is formed in special, meaningful ways. Verbs begin by forming an infinitive: placing "to" in front of a suitable word.

This is the first form of a verb.

*For more details see Form Class Words in the appendix page 103

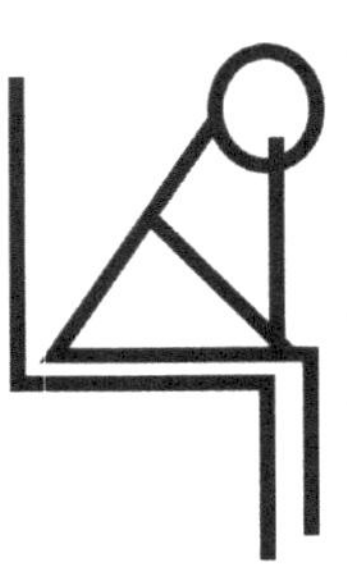# The Infinitive Verb Examples:

Walk, shop or throw would be suitable words to form a verb. Verbs describe movements or links within a sentence

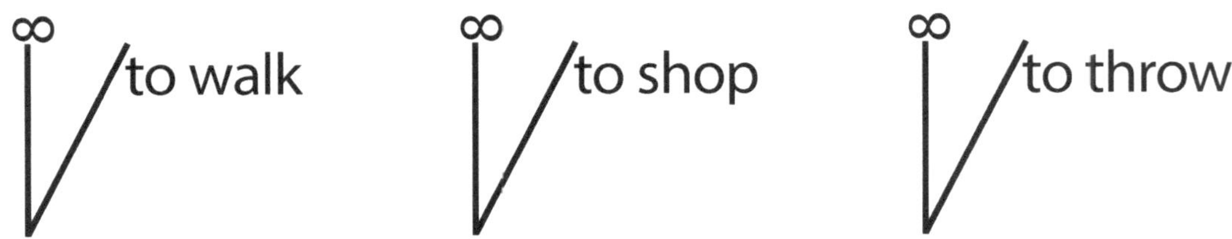

"To" is used to indicate to be done... at any time you like. This form of the verb is timeless. It is neither present, past or furture. The infinity sign is used to show this timeless zone.

PICTURE 19b: The Infinitive Phrase

The infinitive is found in sentences as a phrase, describing movement. It is not the verb.

This is one of the structures derived from a verb.

> " The infinitive phrase describes movement. "

The Infinitive Phrase Examples:

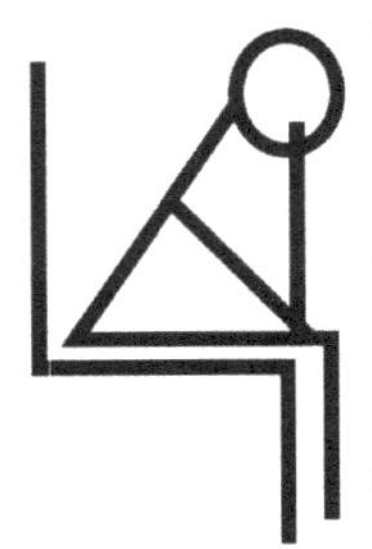

The infinitive is found in sentences as a phrase, describing movement. It is not the verb.

An infinitive can have an object.

It can be handled by an adverb.

An infinitive can have a prepositional phrase.

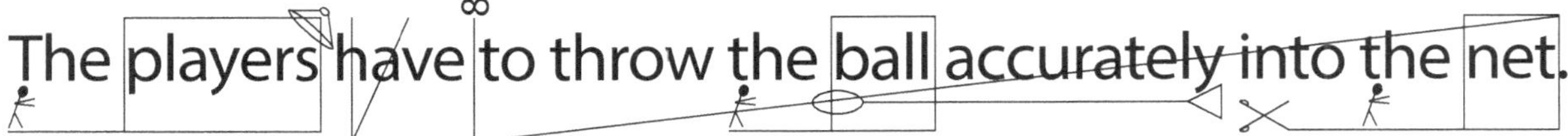

An infinitive can be the main character.

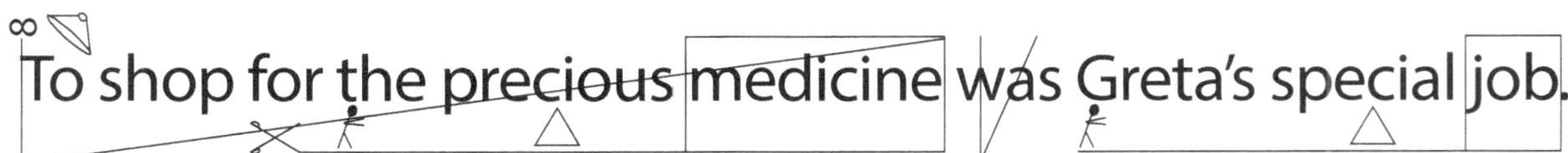

Infinitive Phrase Exercise

Create infinitives by placing "to" before the words that could be used as verbs in this list.

Possible Infinitives

help	see	kitchen
ask	from	experiment
give	freeway	make
play	disaster	furniture

Story 1

Draw the infinitive phrases, include the spotlight and other related Pictures.

To escape was almost impossible. Their plans

to hide on the wharf, to steal a boat and to vanish completely

were crazy. The guards hated to lose any prisoners.

Story 2

Draw the infinitive phrases, include the spotlight and other related Pictures.

To live in a large town was probably nice for Cinderella.

Her chores to shop, to pay the bills and to visit the Post Office

were part of her very busy day.

Infinitive Phrase Answers

Create infinitives by placing "to" before the words that could be used as verbs in this list.

Possible Infinitives

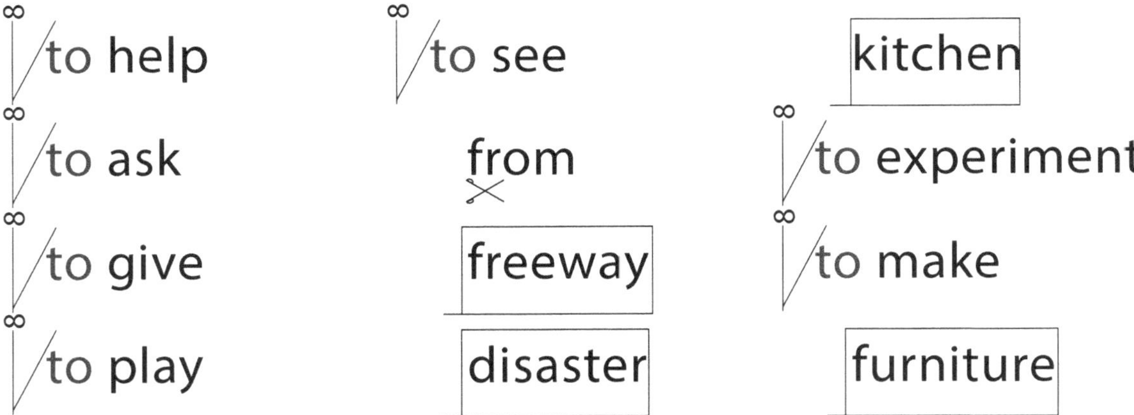

Story 1

Draw the infinitive phrases, include the spotlight and other related Pictures.

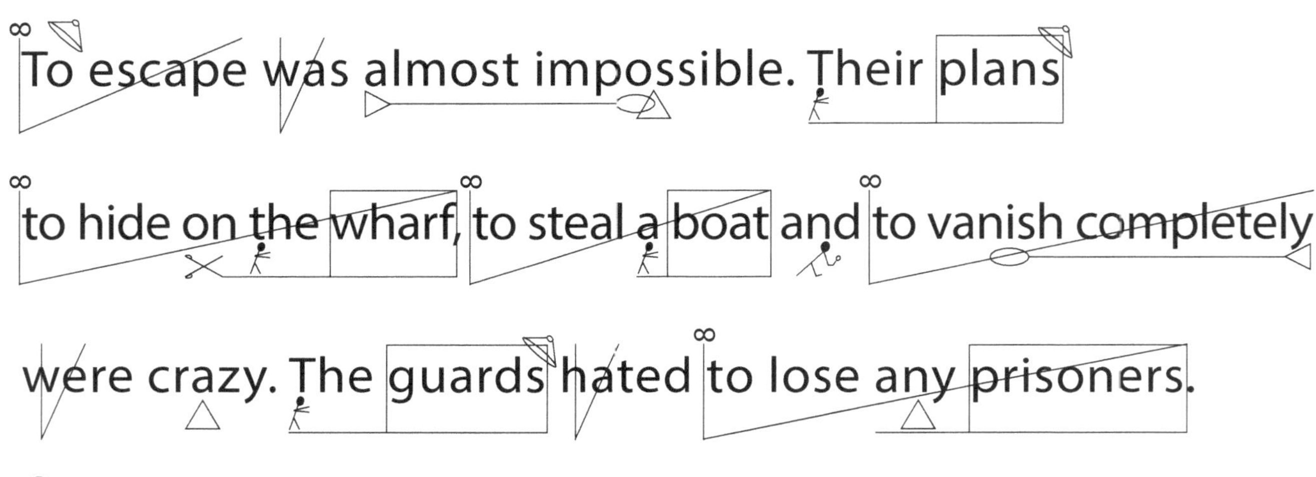

Story 2

Draw the infinitive phrases, include the spotlight and other related Pictures.

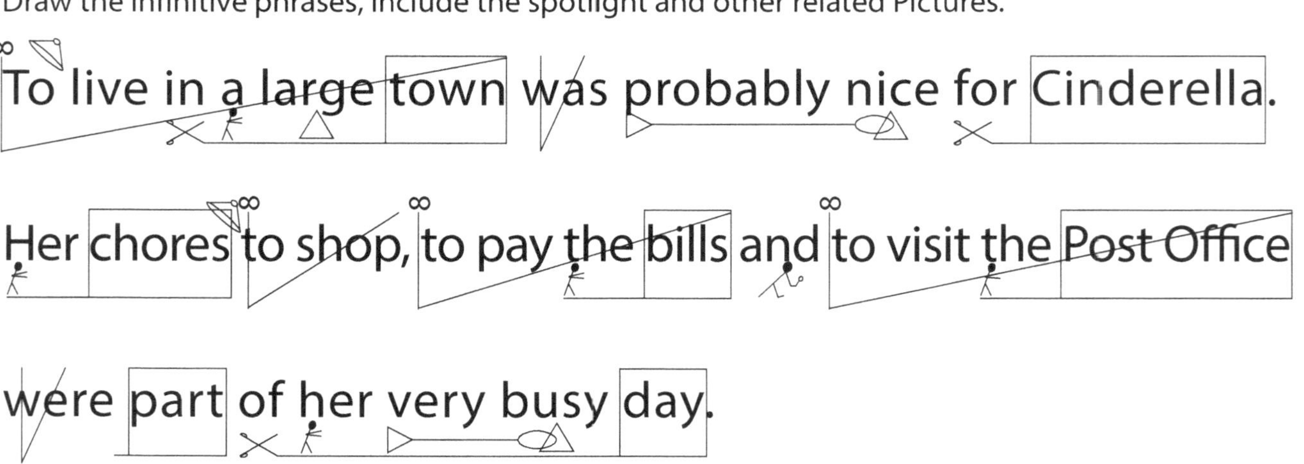

PICTURE 19c: The Present & Past Participle of the Verb

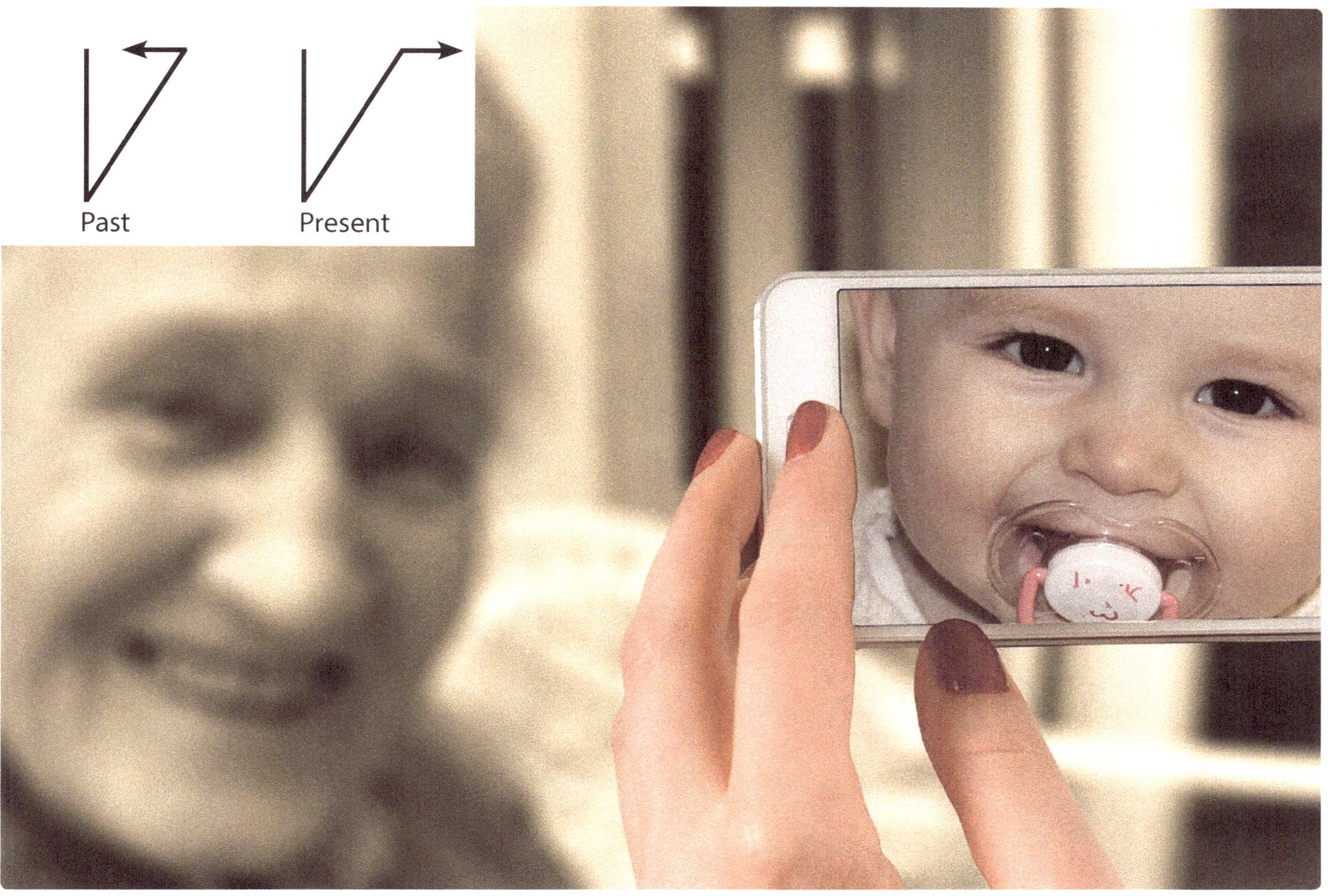

> **"The arrow of the picture tells us if the participle is past or present."**

From the infinitive, the verb can form the present or the past participle.

As a form class word, these are structures formed from a verb.

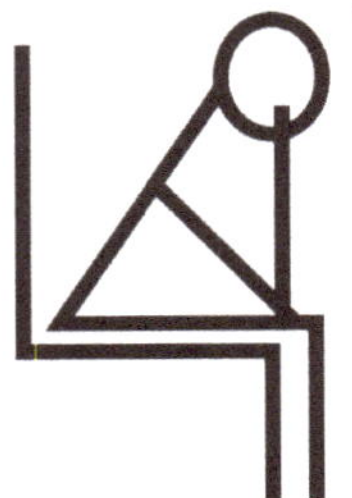# The Present Participle of the Verb
Examples:

In these examples we will be using "to save" and "to chew".

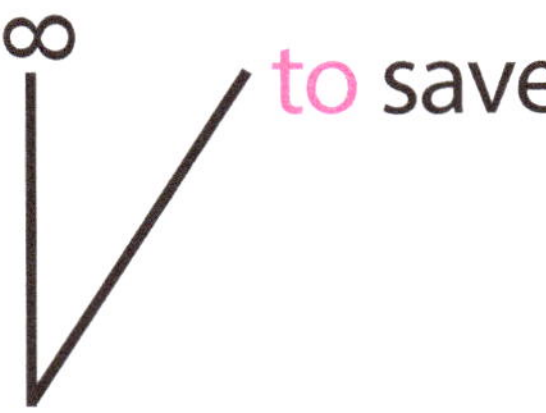

remove to: add (suffix) ing

remove to: add (suffix) ing

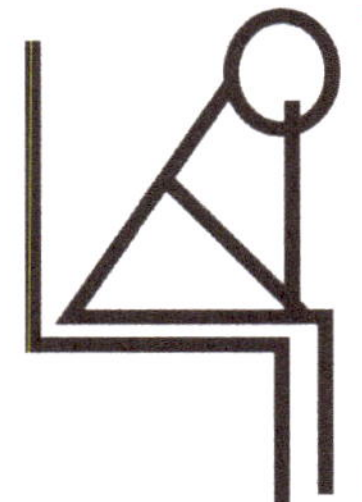# The Past Participle of the Verb
Examples:

In these examples we will be using "to save" and "to chew".

remove to: add (suffix) ed

remove to: add (suffix) ed

The Participle of the Verb Exercise

Create present participles of these verbs by removing to from the infinitive and adding (the suffix) ing

to help ....   to ask ....    to exercise .... 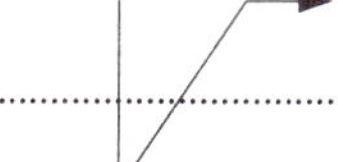

to push ....   to play ....   to scream .... 

to cook ....   to want ....   to invent .... 

Create past participles of these verbs by removing to from the infinitive and adding (the suffix) ed

to help ....   to ask ....    to exercise .... 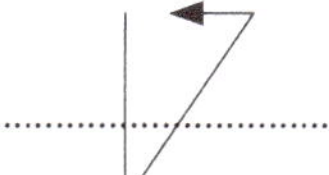

to push ....   to play ....    to scream .... 

to cook ....   to want ....   to invent .... 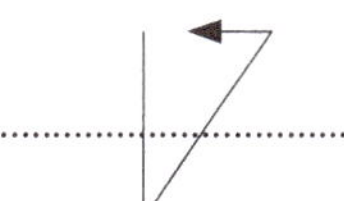

Form the participle according to the Picture.

to look ....   to use .... 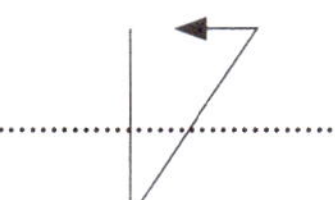   to help .... 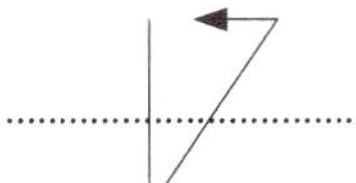

to work ....    to call ....   to ask .... 

to need ....   to start ....   to move .... 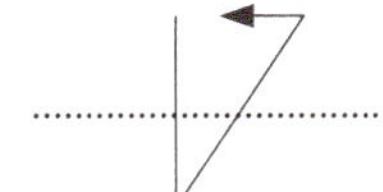

to turn ....   to like .... 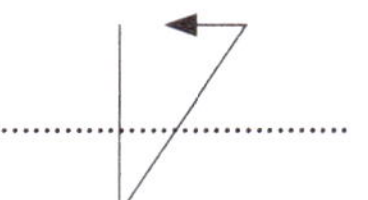   to live .... 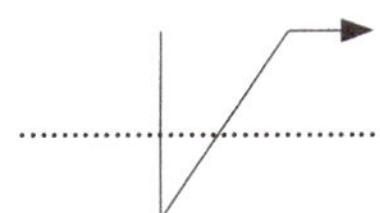

The Participle of the Verb Answers

Create present participles of these verbs by removing to from the infinitive and adding (the suffix) ing

to help	helping	to ask	asking	to exercise	exercising
to push	pushing	to play	playing	to scream	screaming
to cook	cooking	to want	wanting	to invent	inventing

Create past participles of these verbs by removing to from the infinitive and adding (the suffix) ed

to help	helped	to ask	asked	to exercise	exercised
to push	pushed	to play	played	to scream	screamed
to cook	cooked	to want	wanted	to invent	invented

Form the participle according to the Picture.

to look	looked	to use	used	to help	helped
to work	worked	to call	calling	to ask	asking
to need	needed	to start	starting	to move	moved
to turn	turning	to like	liked	to live	living

PICTURE 19d: The Present & Past Participle Phrase

> The participles can be used to begin a phrase called a participle phrase. These participle phrases always act like adjectives, adding information about a noun.
>
> This is one of the structures derived from a verb.

"The arrow of the picture tells us if the participle is past or present."

The Participle Phrase Examples:

A participle phrase can include a noun phrase (the object) and a prepositional phrase.

A participle phrase is not the verb.

The present participle can be used as a noun (as a main character) and can even have a shadow. This is called a gerund.

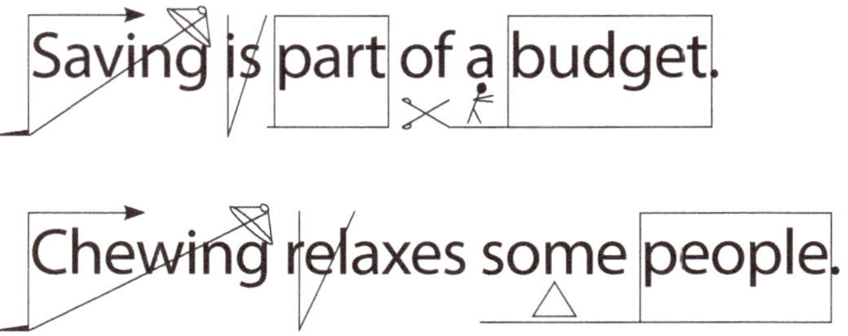

Particles are part of a verb: adverbs can handle them.

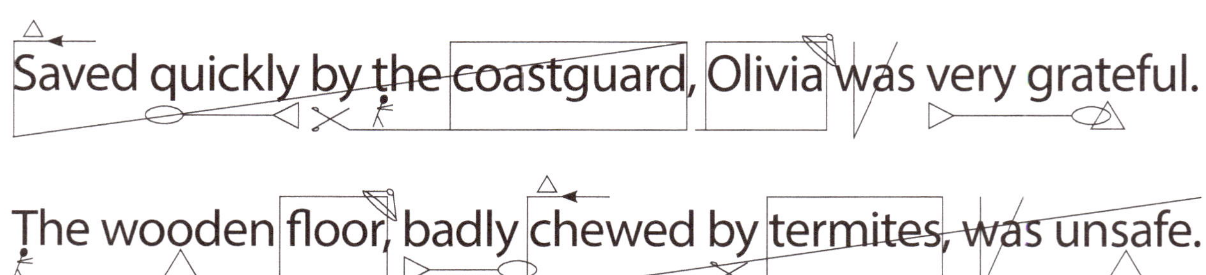

The Participle Phrase Exercise

Complete the present participle phrases by forming the present participle of the suggested verbs. These are not sentences... but interesting ways to begin sentences.

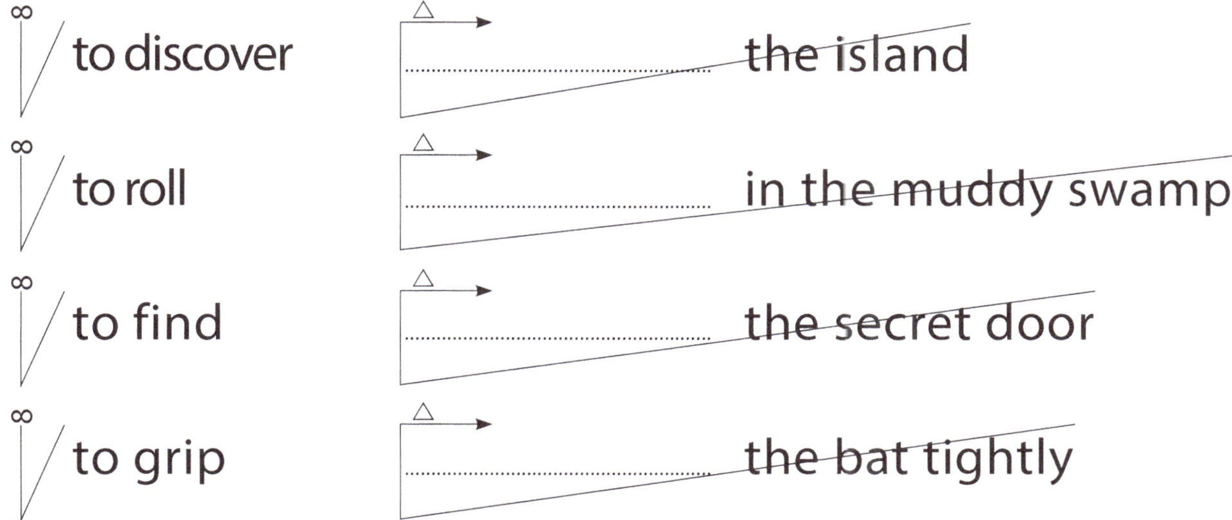

Complete the past participle phrases by forming the past participle of the suggested verbs. These are not sentences... but interesting ways to begin sentences.

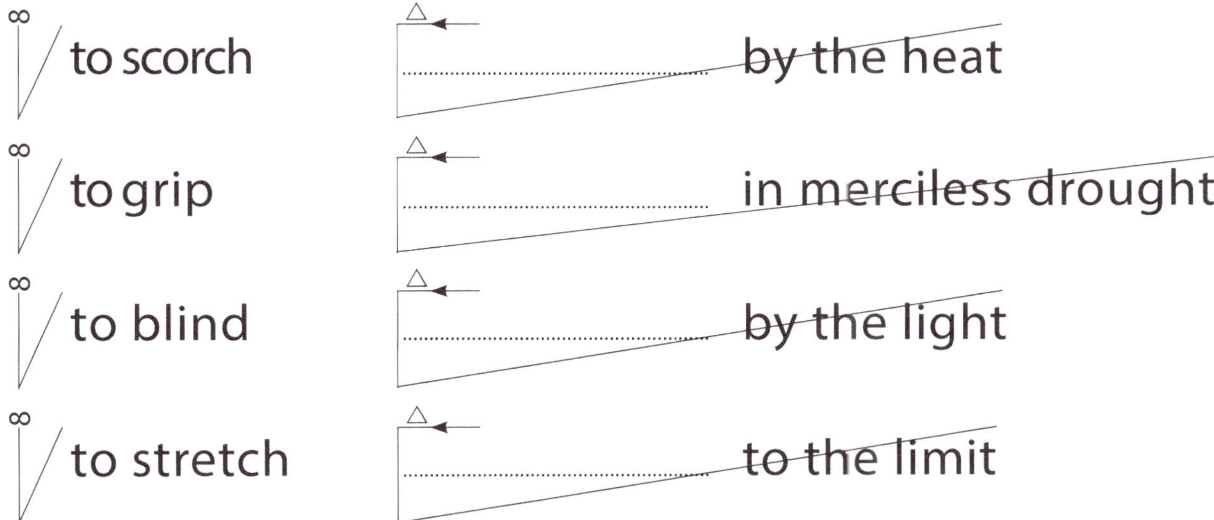

Story with participle phrases (one with an adverb). Always start by boxing the nouns, growing the shadow, and peeking for a preposition.

Excited by the ball, the whole town was feverish. Cooking food, the chefs were busy. Polishing the fancy coaches, the servants were busy. Sewing the gowns, the designers were busy.

Cinderella badly overworked by her sisters was sad.

The Participle Phrase Answers

Complete the present participle phrases by forming the present participle of the suggested verbs. These are not sentences... but interesting ways to begin sentences.

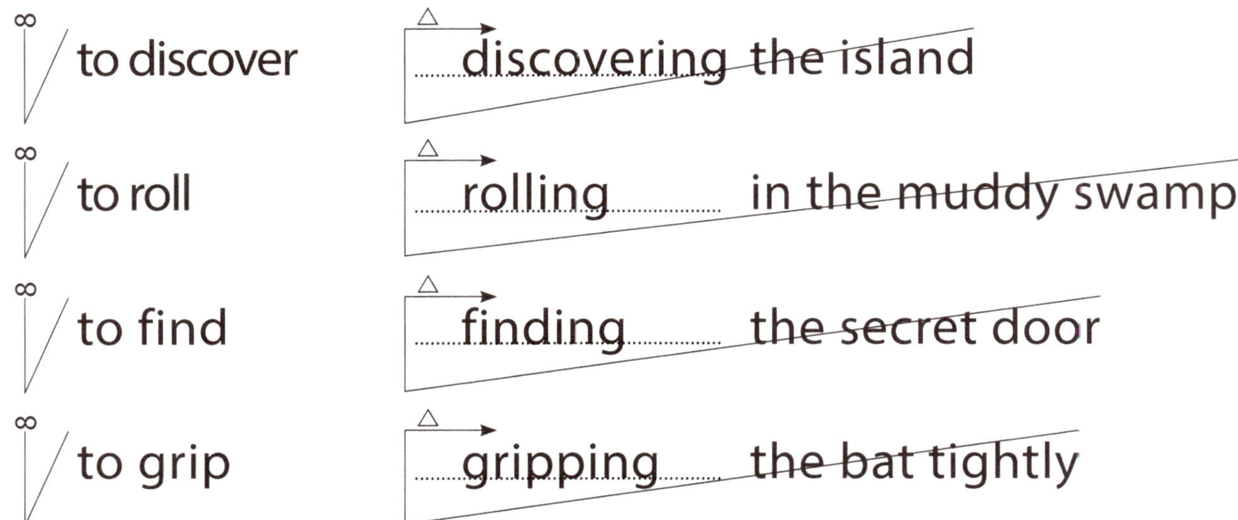

Complete the past participle phrases by forming the past participle of the suggested verbs. These are not sentences... but interesting ways to begin sentences.

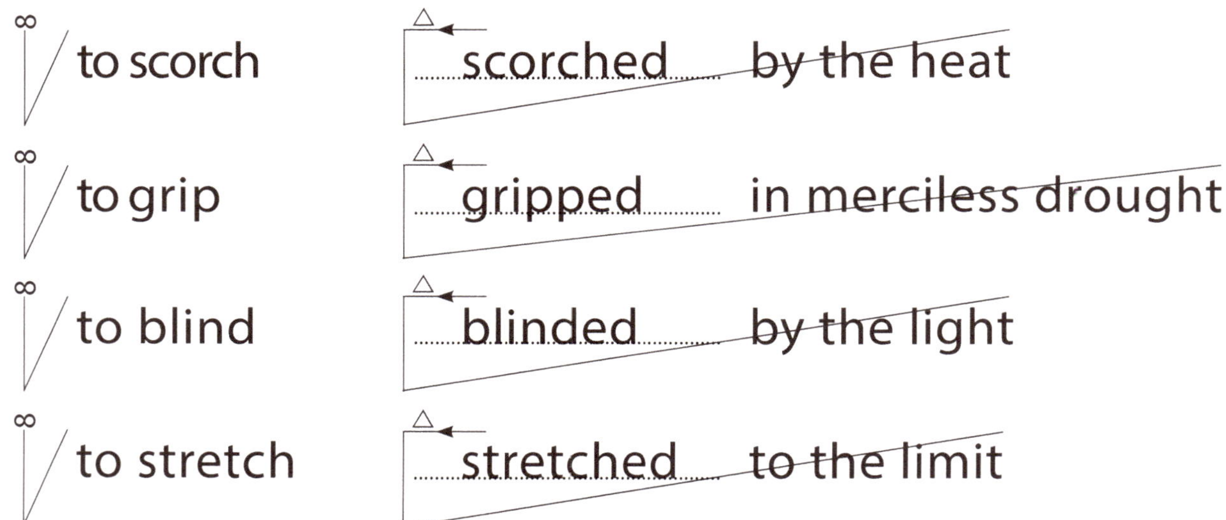

Story with participle phrases (one with an adverb). Always start by boxing the nouns, growing the shadow and peeking for a preposition.

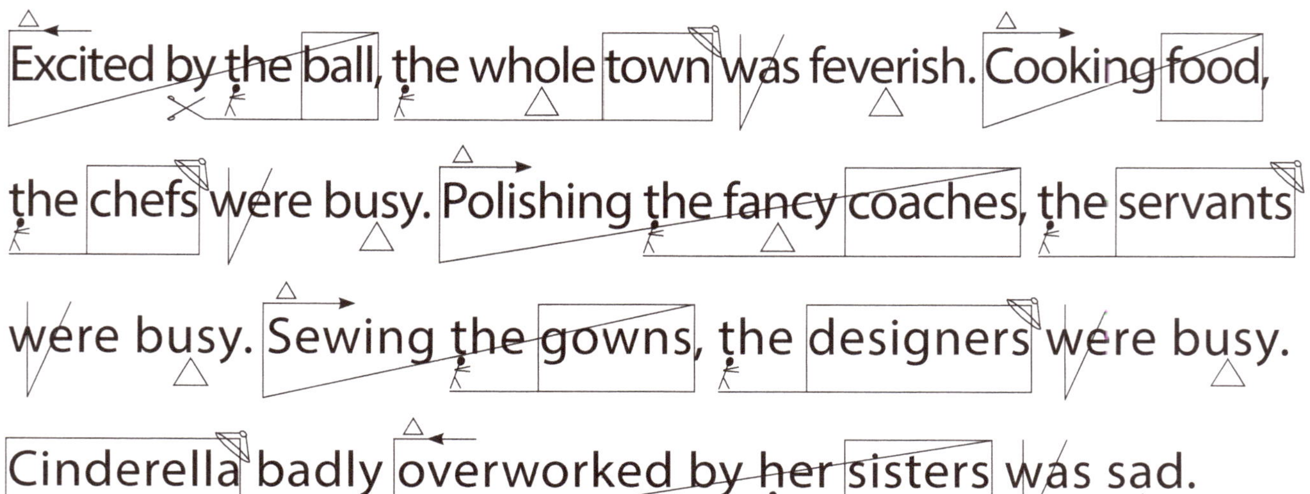

PICTURE 19e: The Present Tense Of The Verb

> **Rediscovering the Present Tense of The Verb from Book 1.**

There are no arrows. It is the present tense or present timezone.

The (simple) present tense is formed by removing "to" from the infinitive and adding an "s" for writing in the third person with single main characters.

The Present Tense of the Verb
Examples:

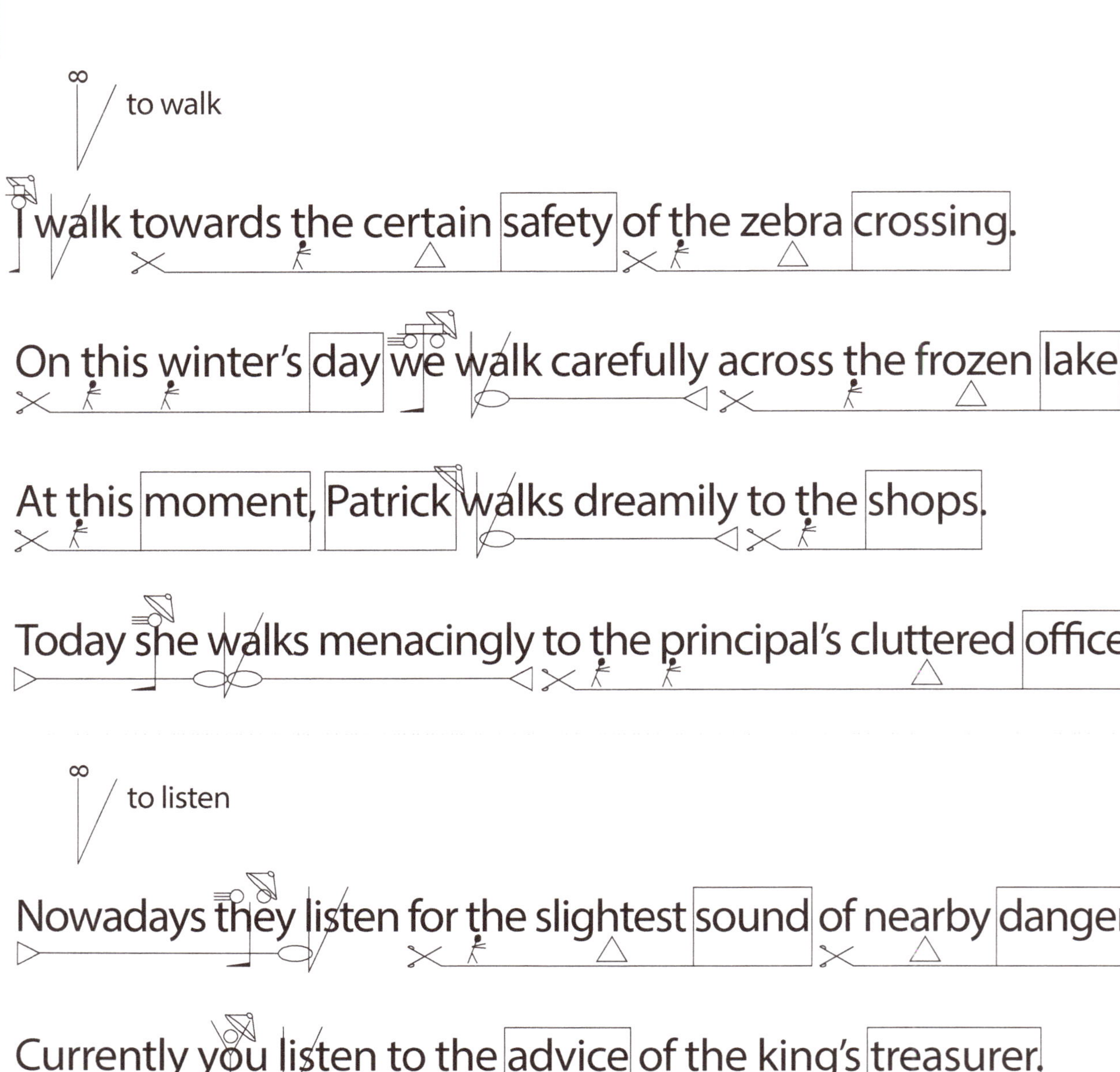

The Present Tense of the Verb

Exercise

Form the (simple) present tense by removing "to" from the infinitives.

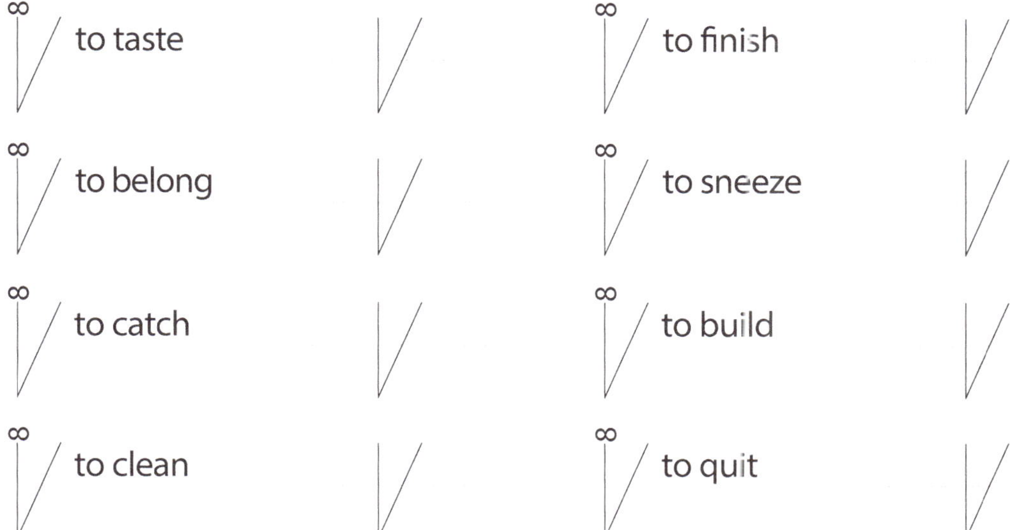

Sentences:

Form the (simple) present tense for these sentences in the third person singular, by removing "to" from the infinitives and then adding (suffix) "s". Draw all the Pictures.

The Present Tense of the Verb

Answers

Form the (simple) present tense by removing "to" from the infinitives.

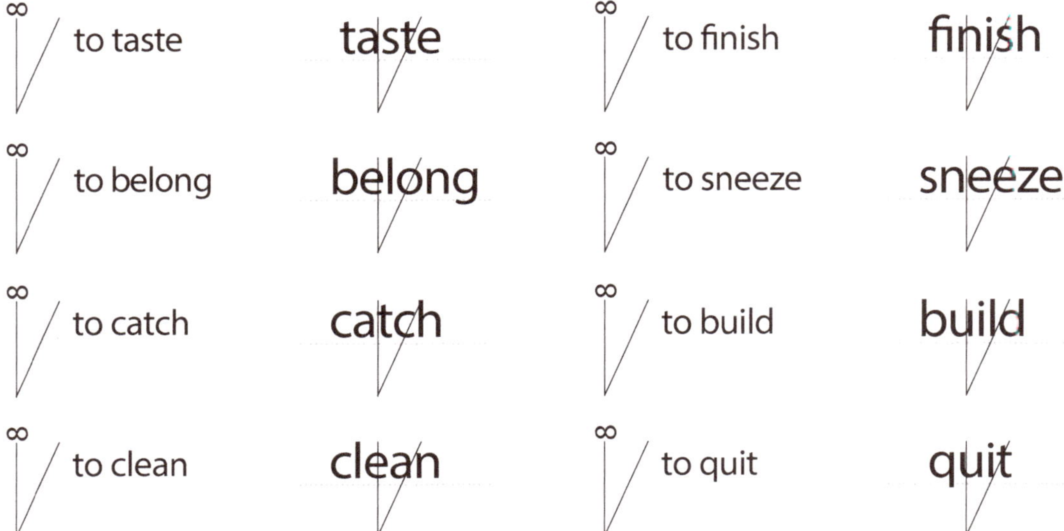

∞ to taste — taste

∞ to finish — finish

∞ to belong — belong

∞ to sneeze — sneeze

∞ to catch — catch

∞ to build — build

∞ to clean — clean

∞ to quit — quit

Sentences:

Form the (simple) present tense for these sentences in the third person singular, by removing "to" from the infinitives and then adding (suffix) "s". Draw all the Pictures.

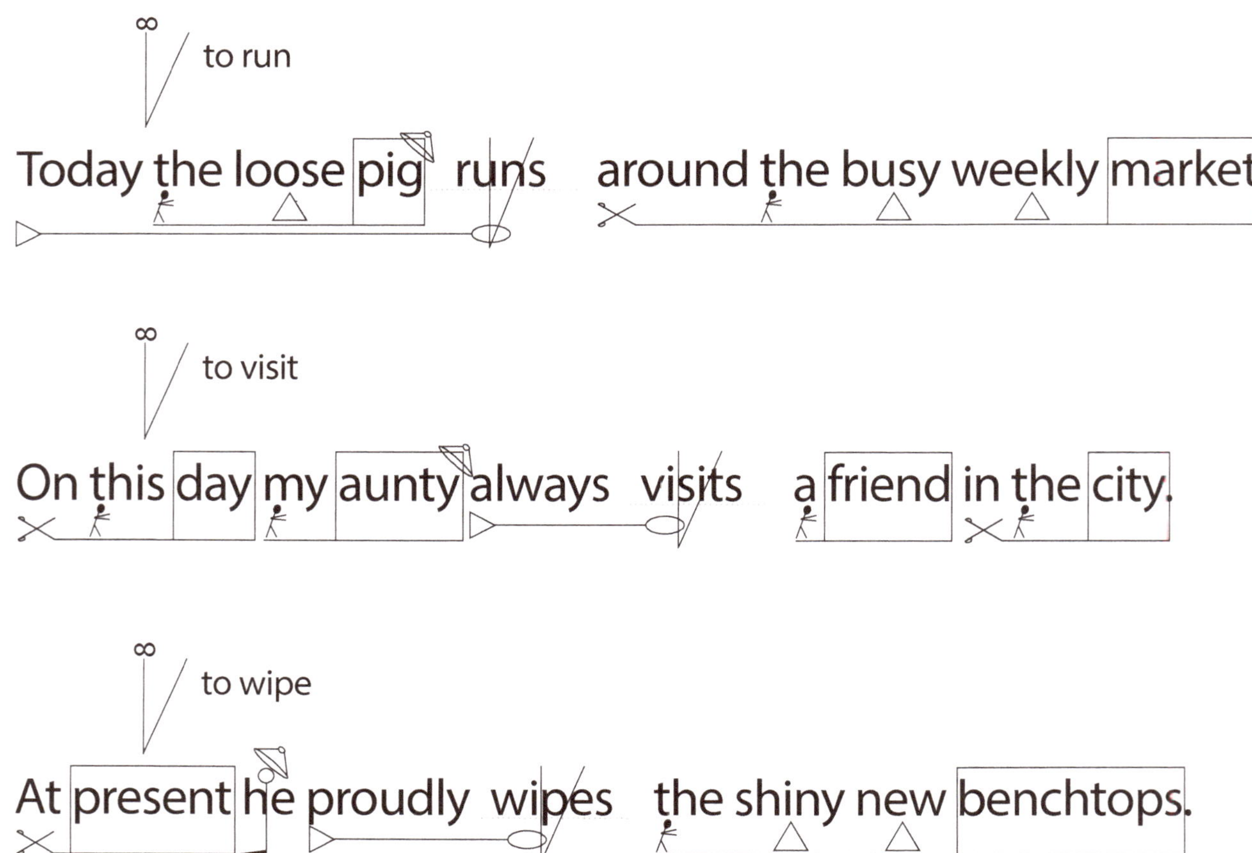

∞ to run

Today the loose pig runs around the busy weekly market.

∞ to visit

On this day my aunty always visits a friend in the city.

∞ to wipe

At present he proudly wipes the shiny new benchtops.

PICTURE 20: The (Subject) Pronoun Pyramid

The form of the verb needs to match the main character (or subject) of the sentence. This is sometimes referred to as the conjugation of the verb.

> " Pronouns replace nouns that are already known to us. "

The (Subject) Pronoun Pyramid
Examples:

The form of the verb needs to match with the main character (or subject) of the sentence. There is a pattern in this matching which can be seen using the pronoun pyramid.

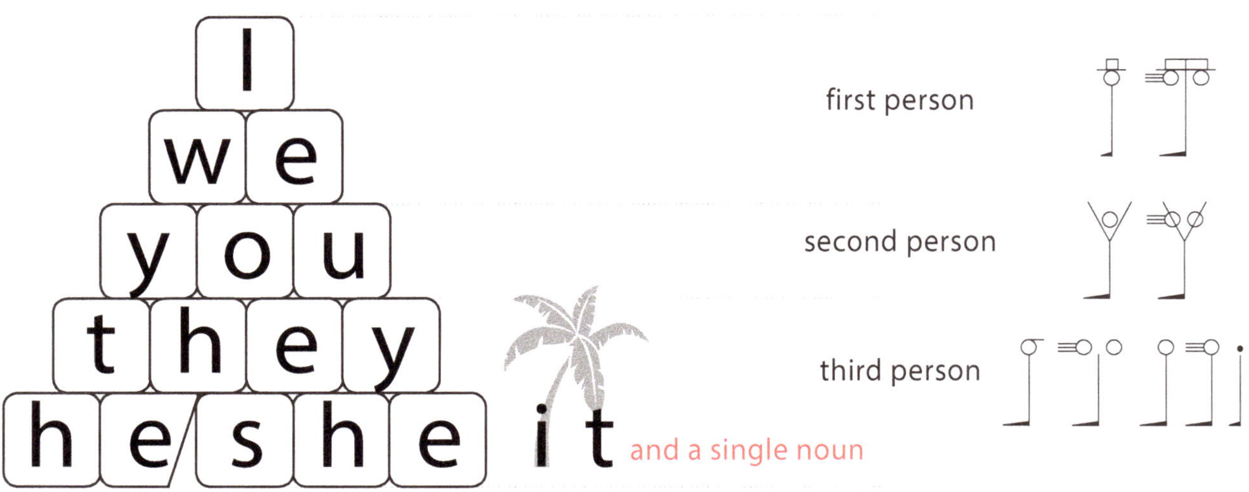

The subject pronoun pyramid: to walk, to look, to help, and to call.

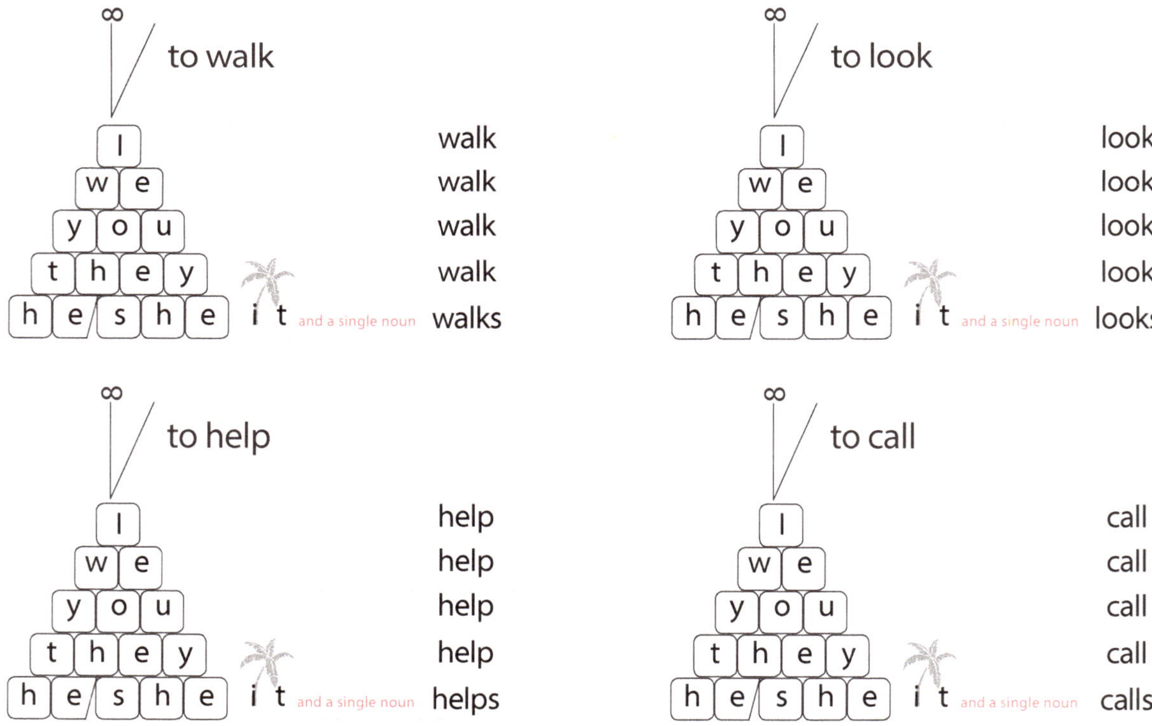

The third person singular is always formed with an "s" suffix.
Some irregular verbs which are more complex will be covered later in the book.

The (Subject) Pronoun Pyramid

Exercise

Create the present tense of the verb from these infinitives. Use the pronoun pyramid to remember the patterns.

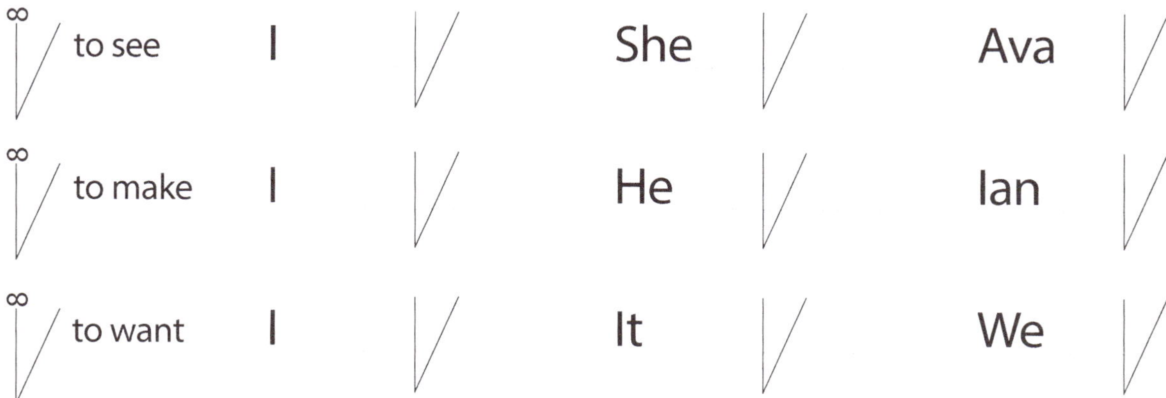

Story 1:

Draw the Picture for the present tense of each verb.

I notice my friends in the park. They play together and the dog plays too. We play happily. I run down the path and the dog runs too.

Story 2:

Identify the present tense of the verbs, a relative pronoun clause, two conjunctions, six prepositional phrases, a noun becoming a determiner and one infinitive phrase.

I watch Cinderella who seems happy with her duties. I walk the busy streets and Cinderella walks the same busy streets. From the castle on the hill the old king looks over the village and worries about his son's future. His son, the prince, needs a wife.

The (Subject) Pronoun Pyramid

Answers

Create the present tense verb from these infinitives. Use the pronoun pyramid to remember the patterns.

∞ to see   I   see   She   sees   Ava   sees

∞ to make   I   make   He   makes   Ian   makes

∞ to want   I   want   It   wants   We   want

Story 1:

Draw the Picture for the present tense of each verb.

I notice my friends in the park. They play together and the dog plays too. We play happily. I run down the path and the dog runs too.

Story 2:

Identify the present tense of the verbs, a relative pronoun clause, two conjunctions, six prepositional phrases, a noun becoming a determiner and one infinitive phrase.

I watch Cinderella who seems happy with her duties. I walk the busy streets and Cinderella walks the same busy streets. From the castle on the hill the old king looks over the village and worries about his son's future. His son, the prince, needs a wife.

PICTURE 19f: The Past Tense Of The Verb

> **Regular verbs just need the suffix "ed" added.**

The Past Tense of the Verb
Examples:

These are regular verbs: just add (the suffix) "ed"

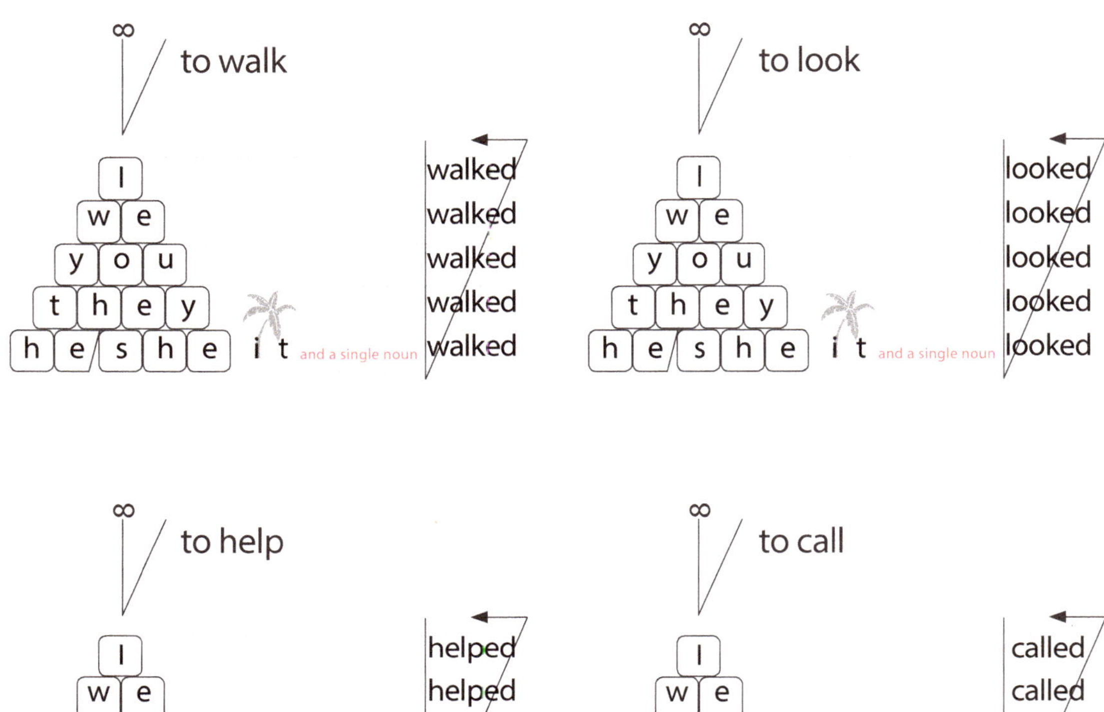

The Past Tense of the Verb Exercises:

Create the past tense with these verbs. Use the pronoun pyramid to remember the pattern.

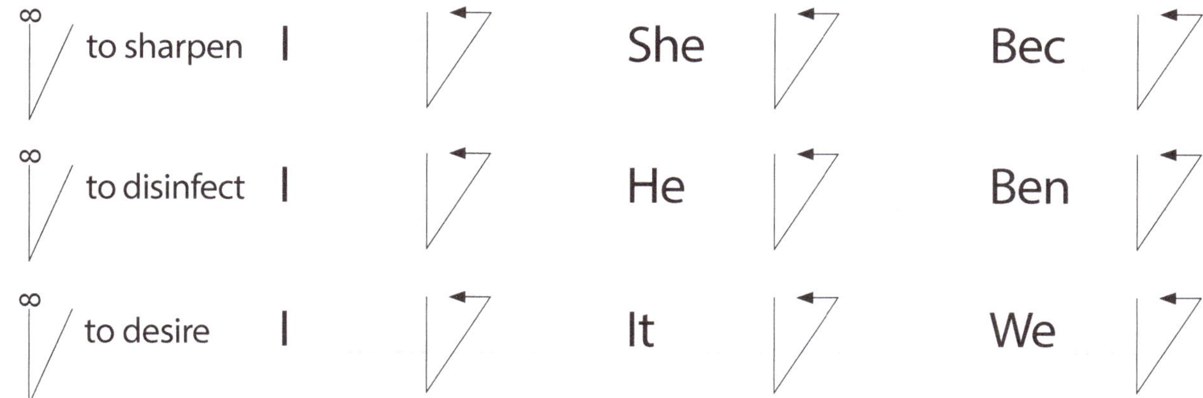

Story 1:

Draw the Picture for the past tense of each verb. (Draw all of the Pictures)

Evelynne planned her day. She made a rough schedule which appeared unbelievable. Her mother wanted groceries.

Her dog demanded a walk and Evelynne's friend needed advice.

Story 2:

Identify the past tense of the verbs, two present participle phrases (one with an adverb), five prepositional phrases (one with a conjunction).

In her narrow room Cinderella dozed. She stirred to the sound of a musical voice. Opening her eyes, Cinderella warily peeked at her open window. Carelessly swinging her legs, an old lady whispered fantastic tales of magically marvellous occurrences.

The Past Tense of the Verb Answers:

Create the past tense with these verbs. Use the pronoun pyramid to remember the pattern.

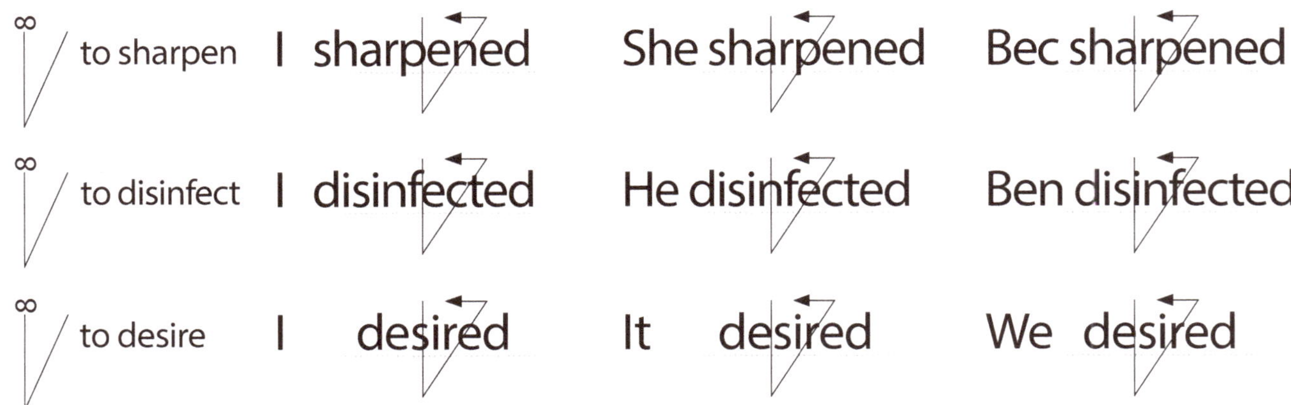

to sharpen   I sharpened   She sharpened   Bec sharpened

to disinfect   I disinfected   He disinfected   Ben disinfected

to desire   I desired   It desired   We desired

Story 1:

Draw the Picture for the past tense of each verb. (Draw all of the Pictures)

Evelynne planned her day. She made a rough schedule which appeared unbelievable. Her mother wanted groceries. Her dog demanded a walk and Evelynne's friend needed advice.

Story 2:

Identify the past tense of the verbs, two present participle phrases (one with an adverb), five prepositional phrases (one with a conjunction).

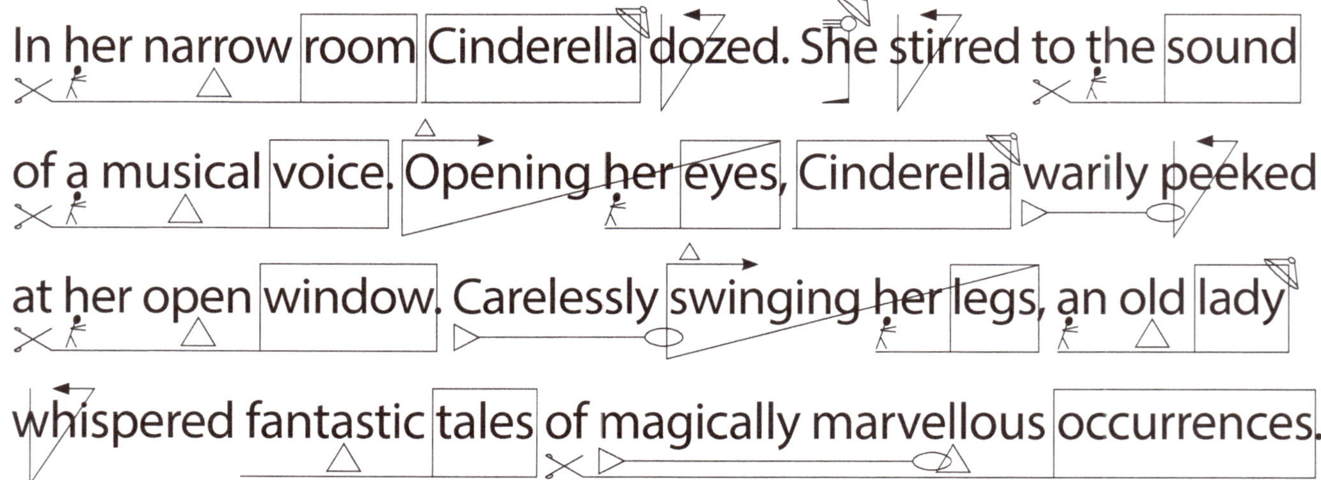

In her narrow room Cinderella dozed. She stirred to the sound of a musical voice. Opening her eyes, Cinderella warily peeked at her open window. Carelessly swinging her legs, an old lady whispered fantastic tales of magically marvellous occurrences.

PICTURE 19f: The Past Tense Of The Verb (Cont.)

Regular and Irregular Verbs

We must consider, with the past tense of the verb, two types of verbs.

These are regular verbs and irregular verbs. The past participle demonstrates the difference.

> " Irregular verbs have no regular pattern when forming the past tense. "

The Past Tense Of The Verb (Cont.) Examples

Regular Verbs

There is a pattern! These are regular verbs because the past participle is formed exactly the same way as the past tense by regularly using the suffix "ed".

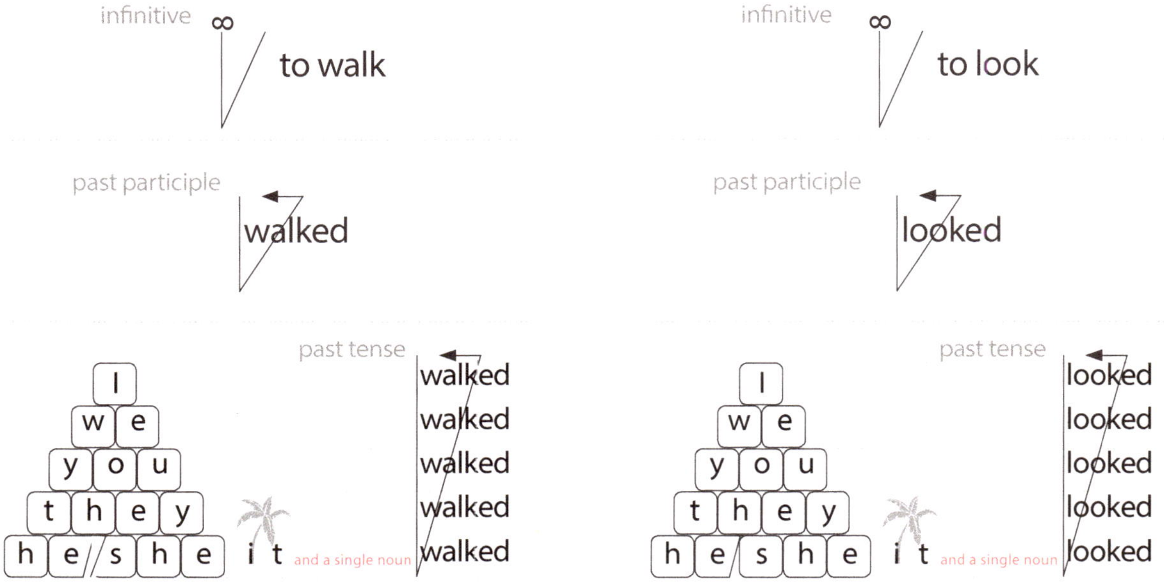

Irregular Verbs

These are irregular verbs. The past participle is formed by morphing the word, and the past tense is also formed by morphing the word, not by regularly using the suffix "ed". Note: Irregular verbs can have different forms for the past participle and past tense.

The Past Tense Of The Verb (Cont.)

Exercise
Irregular Verbs

These are irregular verbs. Match and join by drawing a line between the past participle and the correct infinitive.

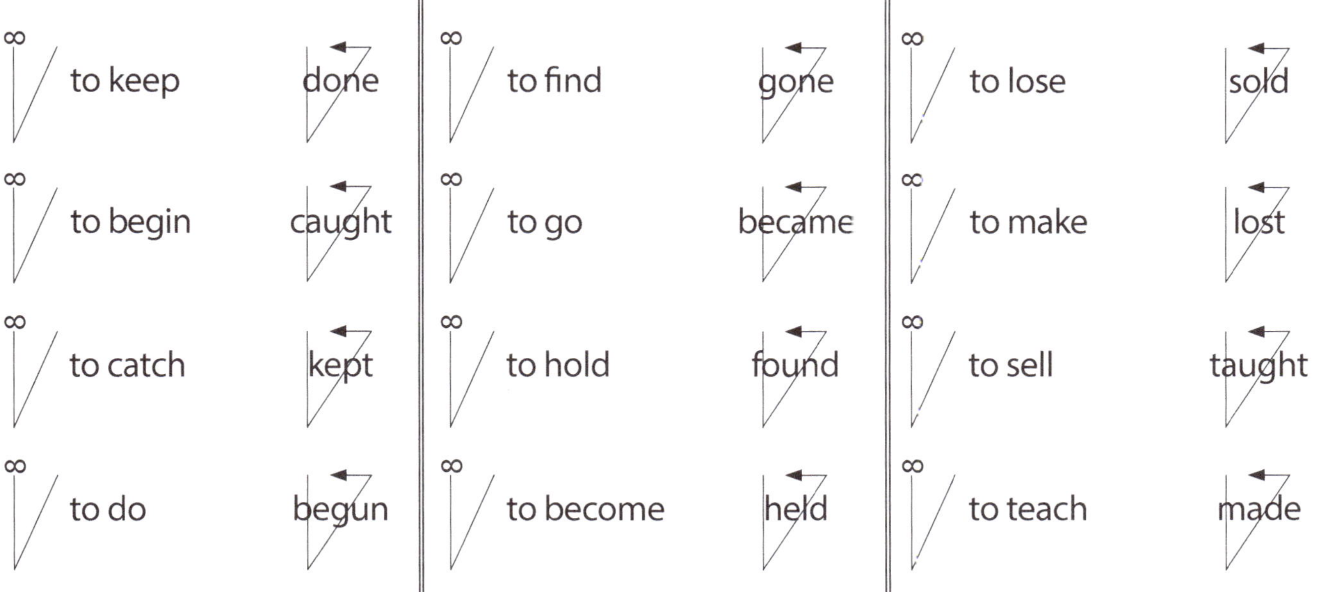

∞ to keep	done	∞ to find	gone	∞ to lose	sold
∞ to begin	caught	∞ to go	became	∞ to make	lost
∞ to catch	kept	∞ to hold	found	∞ to sell	taught
∞ to do	begun	∞ to become	held	∞ to teach	made

Story:

Find all six irregular verbs within the story and write their infinitive form below. Draw in all the other Pictures.

The netballers fought their rivals and became the premiers.

They clung to the trophy and felt like winners. The players

went to a wonderfully special dinner and kept their high spirits.

Write the infinitive form of the verbs within the story with their past tense.

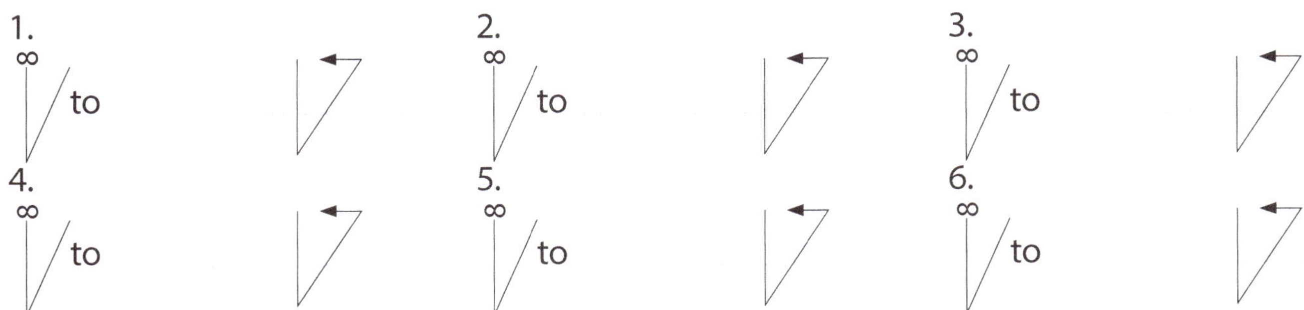

1. ∞ to

2. ∞ to

3. ∞ to

4. ∞ to

5. ∞ to

6. ∞ to

The Past Tense Of The Verb (Cont.)

Answers

Irregular Verbs

These are irregular verbs. Match and join by drawing a line between the past participle and the correct infinitive.

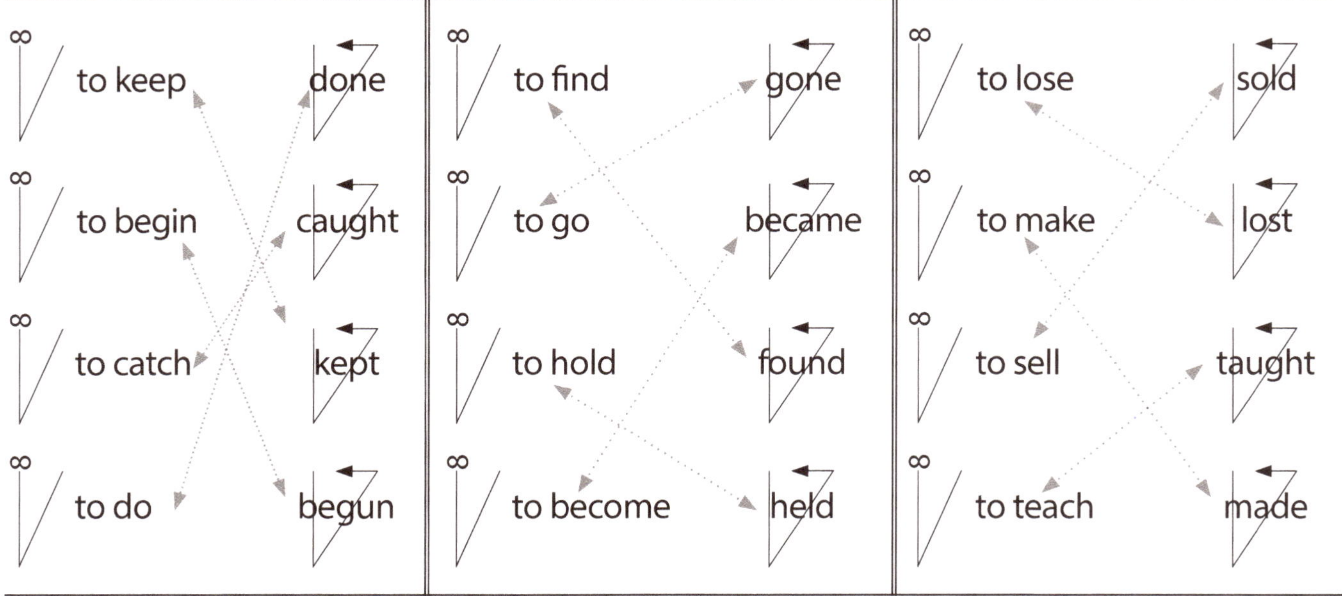

Story:

Find all six irregular verbs within the story and write their infinitive form below. Draw in all the other Pictures.

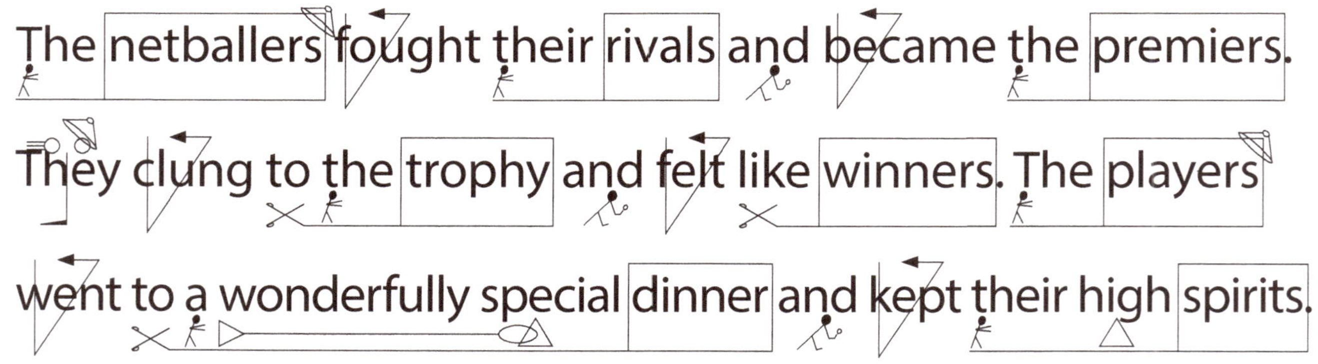

Write the infinitive form of the verbs within the story with their past tense.

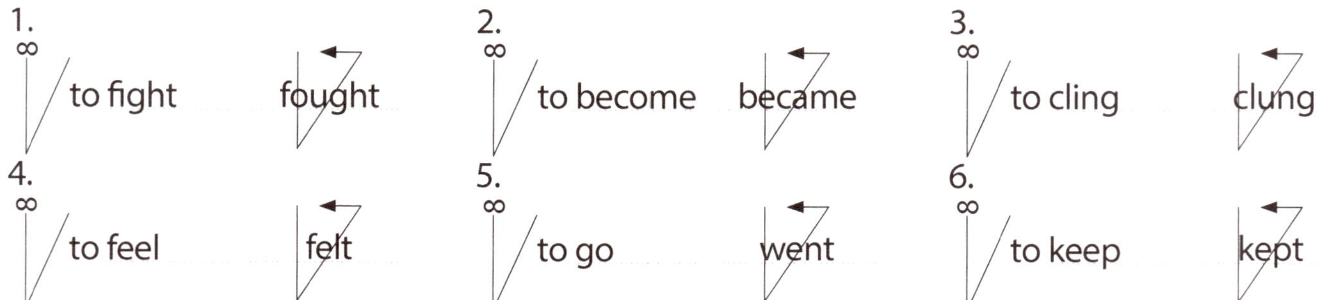

PICTURE 19g: The Most Irregular, Most Used Verb

The Irregular Verb: "to be"

> **The most irregular verb is "to be", made famous by William Shakespeare's Hamlet.**

The irregular verb "to be" does not follow the rules of regular verbs or irregular verbs. It is a unique case.

When you see these words in a sentence, they are verbs, and usually linking verbs (linking the main character to an idea which completes the sentence).

The Most Irregular, Most Used Verb Example

The irregular verb "to be" has a morphed form for each derivative. Only the present participle is consistent with the suffix "ing".

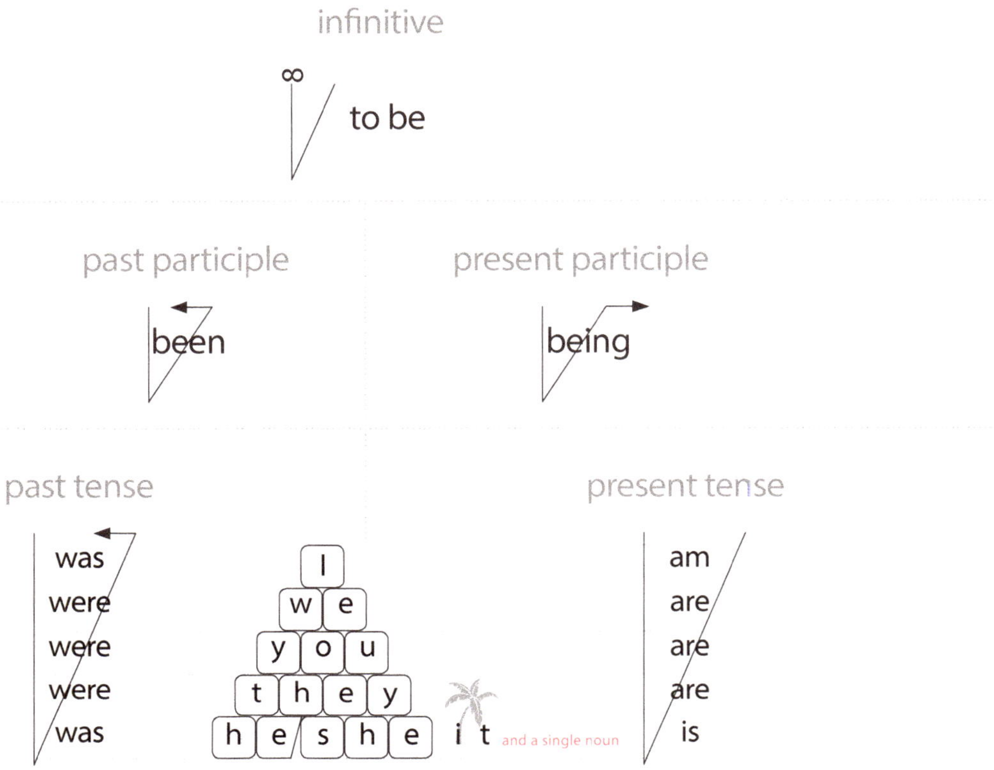

infinitive

to be

past participle

been

present participle

being

past tense

was
were
were
were
was

present tense

am
are
are
are
is

I
we
you
they
he she it and a single noun

I am grateful. Eating porridge yesterday I was ungrateful.

linking   linking

We are famous. On the plane we were unknown.

linking   linking

You are a kind person. You were a brute on the field.

linking   linking

Peter and Gordon are a duo. They were previously soloists.

linking   linking

In the sun Olivia is hot. She was too cold in the mall.

linking   linking

The Most Irregular, Most Used Verb Exercises

Create the present tense of the verb "to be"

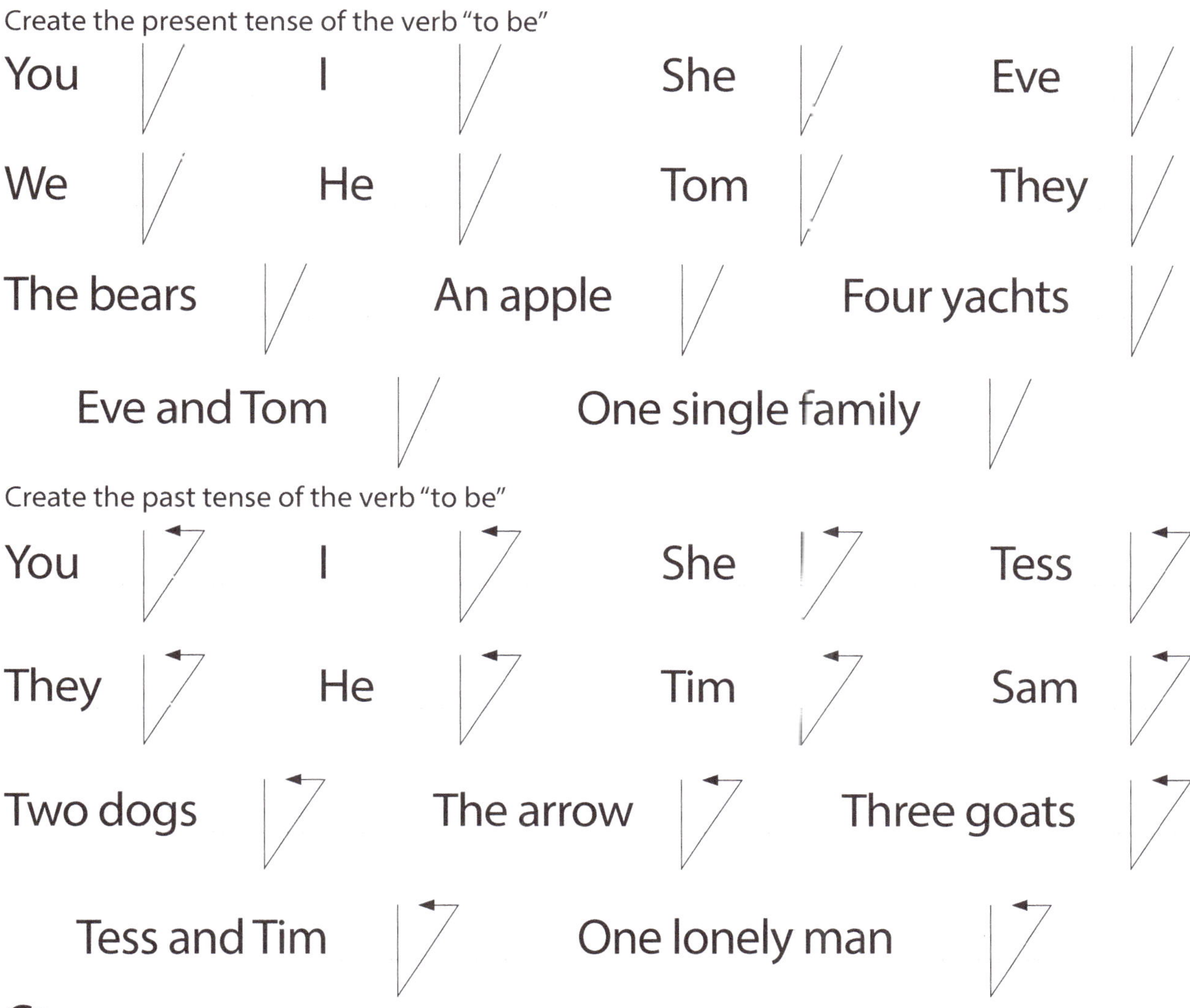

You I She Eve

We He Tom They

The bears An apple Four yachts

Eve and Tom One single family

Create the past tense of the verb "to be"

You I She Tess

They He Tim Sam

Two dogs The arrow Three goats

Tess and Tim One lonely man

Story:

All of the verbs are from "to be". Notice how the verbs link the main character with an adjective or with a noun, to complete the sentence. Write "linking" underneath them. Verbs in the past tense must point to the past.

The classroom is quiet. It was noisy in the morning. The students

are calm in the afternoon. Before lunch they were a rowdy crowd.

I am their teacher. I was their teacher throughout the year.

We are a good combination. Our learning is usually enjoyable.

The Most Irregular, Most Used Verb Answers

Create the present tense of the verb "to be"

You	are	I	am	She	is	Eve	is
We	are	He	is	Tom	is	They	are
The bears	are	An apple	is	Four yachts	are		
Eve and Tom	are	One single family	is				

Create the past tense of the verb "to be"

You	were	I	was	She	was	Tess	was
They	were	He	was	Tim	was	Sam	was
Two dogs	were	The arrow	was	Three goats	were		
Tess and Tim	were	One lonely man	was				

Story:

All of the verbs are from "to be". Notice how the verbs link the main character with an adjective or with a noun, to complete the sentence. Write "linking" underneath them. Verbs in the past tense must point to the past.

The classroom is quiet. It was noisy in the morning. The students are calm in the afternoon. Before lunch they were a rowdy crowd. I am their teacher. I was their teacher throughout the year. We are a good combination. Our learning is usually enjoyable.

(is: linking; are: linking; were: linking; am: linking; was: linking; are: linking; is: linking)

PICTURE 19h: Another Irregular, Most Used Verb

The Irregular Verb: "to have"

> **With "to have", you sensibly need to have... something!
> An "object".**

The irregular verb "to have" is a transitive verb. Transitive verbs have an object: a noun. Transitive verbs are waiting to spot a noun. If you see a transitive verb, you know that a noun is coming.

People who are trainspotters, know that a train is coming. As a reader, when we see a transitive verb we know a noun is coming.

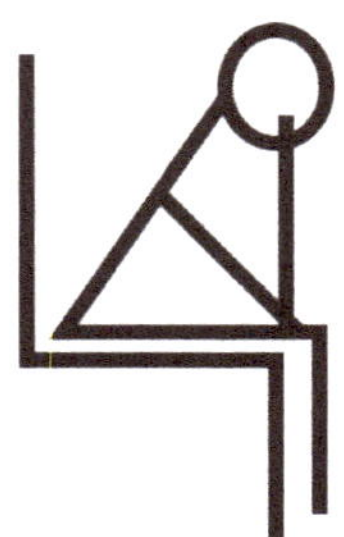

Another Irregular, Most Used Verb Example

The irregular verb "to have" family tree can be seen below. In the examples notice how the verb "to have" is followed by an object.

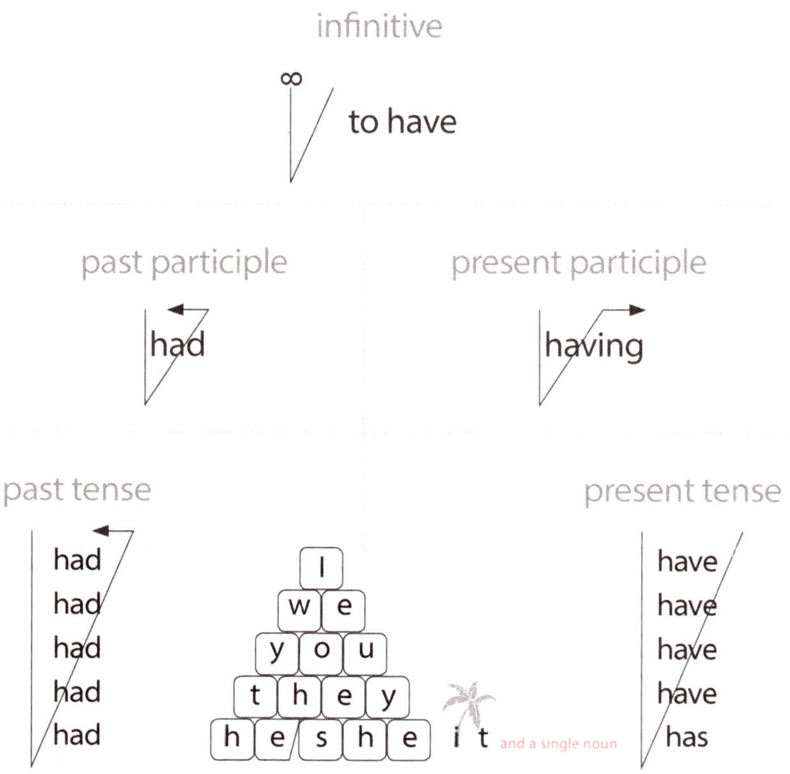

infinitive

to have

past participle

had

present participle

having

past tense

had
had
had
had
had

present tense

have
have
have
have
has

I have a headache. Playing football I had a collision.

trans object   trans object

We have many presents. On Sunday we had a family party.

trans object   trans object

You have a magnificent house. You had a rich uncle.

trans object   trans object

Peter and Mary have a gold award. They had a hit song.

trans object   trans object

Maddy has a roomy office. She had many jobs.

trans object   trans object

Another Irregular, Most Used Verb
Exercises

In this exercise, the writing is in the third person, using the transitive verb, "to have". The sentences are either in present tense or past tense. Make sure to use the arrow pointing to the past when showing the past tense of a verb. Draw all of the Pictures, writing "trans" underneath the verb. The verb is expecting an object (usually a noun), but sometimes this noun spot is taken by a phrase. Write "object" in the appropriate spot.

Sentences

Ty has wonderfully long summer holidays.

The clever superheros constantly have to outwit the sly evildoers.

The bridesmaids traditionally had to wear closely similar outfits.

Tung consistently had a mild curry.

The cartoon wolf repeatedly has horrifically bad days.

They seriously have to collect every chocolate cupcake recipe.

Pip has a very tight schedule.

Deb and Di had expensive city apartments.

The bankers generally had the money.

Hans regularly had fast food.

The recyclers had boxes and cans.

Another Irregular, Most Used Verb

Answers

In this exercise, the writing is in the third person, using the transitive verb, "to have". The sentences are either in present tense or past tense. Make sure to use the arrow pointing to the past when showing the past tense of a verb. Draw all of the Pictures, writing "trans" underneath the verb. The verb is expecting an object (usually a noun), but sometimes this noun spot is taken by a phrase. Write "object" in the appropriate spot.

Sentences

Ty has wonderfully long summer holidays.
trans object

The clever superheros constantly have to outwit the sly evildoers.
trans object

The bridesmaids traditionally had to wear closely similar outfits.
trans object

Tung consistently had a mild curry.
trans object

The cartoon wolf repeatedly has horrifically bad days.
trans object

They seriously have to collect every chocolate cupcake recipe.
trans object

Pip has a very tight schedule.
trans object

Deb and Di had expensive city apartments.
trans object

The bankers generally had the money.
trans object

Hans regularly had fast food.
trans object

The recyclers had boxes and cans.
trans object

ADDITIONAL EXERCISES

Keep connecting with the Pictures. Keep practising the patterns.

> " **Exercises can strengthen the mind.** "

Additional Exercise (1)

SEEK & DRAW: Find the structure, draw the Picture.

1. Leaving the barren desert Amara followed the long camel train

2. through the narrow opening within the thick walls into the city.

3. The camels were weary. Their humps were shrunken yet

4. lashed to their harnesses the saddlebags bulged with riches.

5. The wealth of the world rested briefly in this shadowy courtyard.

6. Amara eagerly joined the traders who walked to the busy market.

7. She loved to wander slowly amongst the wonderfully exotic stalls.

8. She liked to smell the foreign unfamiliar fragrances of the East.

9. Amara wanted to taste the unusual foods from faraway places.

10. Amara smiled. She laughed. She searched her pockets for coins.

11. Covered in a spicy sauce chunks of skewered meat sizzled

12. on a thin metal cooktop above a bed of glowing embers.

Additional Exercise (1) Cont.

Seek List:

Line 1. begins with a present participle phrase, (with an object); do all of the Pictures

Line 2. three prepositional phrases

Line 3. a verb from "to be" used twice, and a conjunction

Line 4. begins with a past participle phrase, includes a prepositional phrase; do all the Pictures.

Line 5. two prepositional phrases, a verb handled by an adverb

Line 6. do all of the images (there is a relative pronoun clause)

Line 7. an infinitive phrase handled by an adverb, and includes a prepositional phrase

Line 8. an infinitive phrase with an object

Line 9. an infinitive phrase with an object

Line 10. do all the images

Line 11. a past participle phrase which includes a prepositional phrase

Line 12. three prepositional phrases

Additional Exercise (1) Answers

SEEK & DRAW: Find the structure, draw the Picture.

1. Leaving the barren desert Amara followed the long camel train

2. through the narrow opening within the thick walls into the city.

3. The camels were weary. Their humps were shrunken yet

4. lashed to their harnesses the saddlebags bulged with riches.

5. The wealth of the world rested briefly in this shadowy courtyard.

6. Amara eagerly joined the traders who walked to the busy market.

7. She loved to wander slowly amongst the wonderfully exotic stalls.

8. She liked to smell the foreign unfamiliar fragrances of the East.

9. Amara wanted to taste the unusual foods from faraway places.

10. Amara smiled. She laughed. She searched her pockets for coins.

11. Covered in a spicy sauce chunks of skewered meat sizzled

12. on a thin metal cooktop above a bed of glowing embers.

Additional Exercise (1) Cont.

Seek List:

Line 1. begins with a present participle phrase, (with an object); do all of the Pictures

Line 2. three prepositional phrases

Line 3. a verb from "to be" used twice, and a conjunction

Line 4. begins with a past participle phrase, includes a prepositicnal phrase; do all the Pictures.

Line 5. two prepositional phrases, a verb handled by an adverb

Line 6. do all of the images (there is a relative pronoun clause)

Line 7. an infinitive phrase handled by an adverb, and includes a prepositional phrase

Line 8. an infinitive phrase with an object

Line 9. an infinitive phrase with an object

Line 10. do all the images

Line 11. a past participle phrase which includes a prepositional phrase

Line 12. three prepositional phrases

Additional Exercise (2)

SEEK & DRAW: Find the structure, draw the Picture.

1. Drew parked his vehicle, a red car with the basic accessories,

2. at the top of the cliffs near their edge behind a broken safety rail.

3. Marvelling at the ocean's vastness his gaze swept to the horizon.

4. He relaxed. He listened. Drew belonged to these wild places.

5. Travelling on rough weathered tracks, sleeping under the stars,

6. Drew surfed the desolate coastlines of the Great Australian Bite.

7. Excited by his freedom, Drew grabbed his favourite board and

8. confidently made his way down the zigzagging trail to the beach.

9. To feel the might of the waves and to control their strength

10. was his only ambition. A pod of dolphins seemed a welcome sign.

11. Gulls which roosted in the pock-marked sandstone crags

12. voiced a raucous greeting. Drew gave his usual lopsided smile.

Additional Exercise (2) Cont.

Seek List:

Line 1. past tense of "to park", two noun phrases, and a prepositional phrase

Line 2. four prepositional phrases

Line 3. begins with a present participle phrase which includes a prepositional phrase, the past tense of "to sweep", end with a prepositional phrase, show the main character (subject)

Line 4. a subject pronoun used twice, the past tense of three verbs, draw all the Pictures for the third sentence

Line 5. two present participle phrases, each with a prepositional phrase

Line 6. do all the Pictures

Line 7. begins with a past participle phrase, do all the Pictures

Line 8. an adverb handling a verb, do all the Pictures

Line 9. two infinitive phrases, each with an object and one with a prepositional phrase

Line 10. do all the Pictures for the second sentence

Line 11. a relative pronoun clause

Line 12. do all the Pictures

Additional Exercise (2) Answers

SEEK & DRAW: Find the structure, draw the Picture.

1. Drew parked his vehicle, a red car with the basic accessories,

2. at the top of the cliffs near their edge behind a broken safety rail.

3. Marvelling at the ocean's vastness his gaze swept to the horizon.

4. He relaxed. He listened. Drew belonged to these wild places.

5. Travelling on rough weathered tracks, sleeping under the stars,

6. Drew surfed the desolate coastlines of the Great Australian Bite.

7. Excited by his freedom, Drew grabbed his favourite board and

8. confidently made his way down the zigzagging trail to the beach.

9. To feel the might of the waves and to control their strength

10. was his only ambition. A pod of dolphins seemed a welcome sign.

11. Gulls which roosted in the pock-marked sandstone crags

12. voiced a raucous greeting. Drew gave his usual lopsided smile.

Additional Exercise (2) Cont.

Seek List:

Line 1. past tense of "to park", two noun phrases, and a prepositional phrase

Line 2. four prepositional phrases

Line 3. begins with a present participle phrase which includes a prepositional phrase, the past tense of "to sweep", end with a prepositional phrase, show the main character (subject)

Line 4. a subject pronoun used twice, the past tense of three verbs, draw all the Pictures for the third sentence

Line 5. two present participle phrases, each with a prepositional phrase

Line 6. do all the Pictures

Line 7. begins with a past participle phrase, do all the Pictures

Line 8. an adverb handling a verb, do all the Pictures

Line 9. two infinitive phrases, each with an object and one with a prepositional phrase

Line 10. do all the Pictures for the second sentence

Line 11. a relative pronoun clause

Line 12. do all the Pictures

Additional Exercise (3)

SEEK & DRAW: Find the structure, draw the Picture.

1. Jafari awoke before the dawn's light in Mozambique. He yawned.

2. He stretched. Jafari counted his blessings. He loved his family.

3. Jafari's mother was beautiful. Keeping food on the wooden table

4. his father successfully farmed their small holding of fertile land.

5. Jafari had three sisters and Jafari's grandfather was a toy-maker.

6. Sheltered in the cool the old grandfather picked over his treasures,

7. odds-and-ends which emerged from the village's unwanted goods.

8. In grandfather's hands they became dolls, animals and tiny trucks.

9. To attend school was the most wonderful part of Jafari's long day.

10. To walk for eight kilometres seemed a small task in his routine.

11. To sit in the maths lessons watching the pattern of numbers

12. was more important. Science looked like a great adventure.

Additional Exercise (3) Cont.

Seek List:

Line 1. do all the Pictures

Line 2. do all the Pictures

Line 3. the second sentence begins with a present participle phrase, it has an object and a prepositional phrase

Line 4. do all the Pictures

Line 5. do all the Pictures

Line 6. a past participle phrase including a prepositional phrase, do all the Pictures

Line 7. relative pronoun clause, including a prepositional phrase

Line 8. begins with a prepositional phrase, do all the Pictures

Line 9. begins with an infinitive phrase (it has an object) as the main character, do all the Pictures

Line 10. begins with an infinitive phrase, (it has a prepositional phrase) as the main character, do all the Pictures.

Line 11. begins with an infinitive phrase, (it has a prepositional phrase) as the main character, a present participle phrase, do all the Pictures

Line 12. do all the Pictures

Additional Exercise (3) Answers

SEEK & DRAW: Find the structure, draw the Picture.

1. Jafari awoke before the dawn's light in Mozambique. He yawned.

2. He stretched. Jafari counted his blessings. He loved his family.

3. Jafari's mother was beautiful. Keeping food on the wooden table

4. his father successfully farmed their small holding of fertile land.

5. Jafari had three sisters and Jafari's grandfather was a toy-maker.

6. Sheltered in the cool the old grandfather picked over his treasures,

7. odds-and-ends which emerged from the village's unwanted goods.

8. In grandfather's hands they became dolls, animals and tiny trucks.

9. To attend school was the most wonderful part of Jafari's long day.

10. To walk for eight kilometres seemed a small task in his routine.

11. To sit in the maths lessons watching the pattern of numbers

12. was more important. Science looked like a great adventure.

■ Additional Exercise (3) Cont.

Seek List:

Line 1. do all the Pictures

Line 2. do all the Pictures

Line 3. the second sentence begins with a present participle phrase, it has an object and a prepositional phrase

Line 4. do all the Pictures

Line 5. do all the Pictures

Line 6. a past participle phrase including a prepositional phrase, do all the Pictures

Line 7. relative pronoun clause, including a prepositional phrase

Line 8. begins with a prepositional phrase, do all the Pictures

Line 9. begins with an infinitive phrase (it has an object) as the main character, do all the Pictures

Line 10. begins with an infinitive phrase, (it has a prepositional phrase) as the main character, do all the Pictures.

Line 11. begins with an infinitive phrase, (it has a prepositional phrase) as the main character, a present participle phrase, do all the Pictures

Line 12. do all the Pictures

Additional Exercise (4)

Design & Build Your Own Subject Pronoun Pyramid:
Cut along the dotted lines and glue the flaps to their corresponding position to create a square based pyramid. As a bonus, before folding and glueing, you may chose to colour it in. Once it is together, you might put it on display to help you remember the subject pronouns and their use.

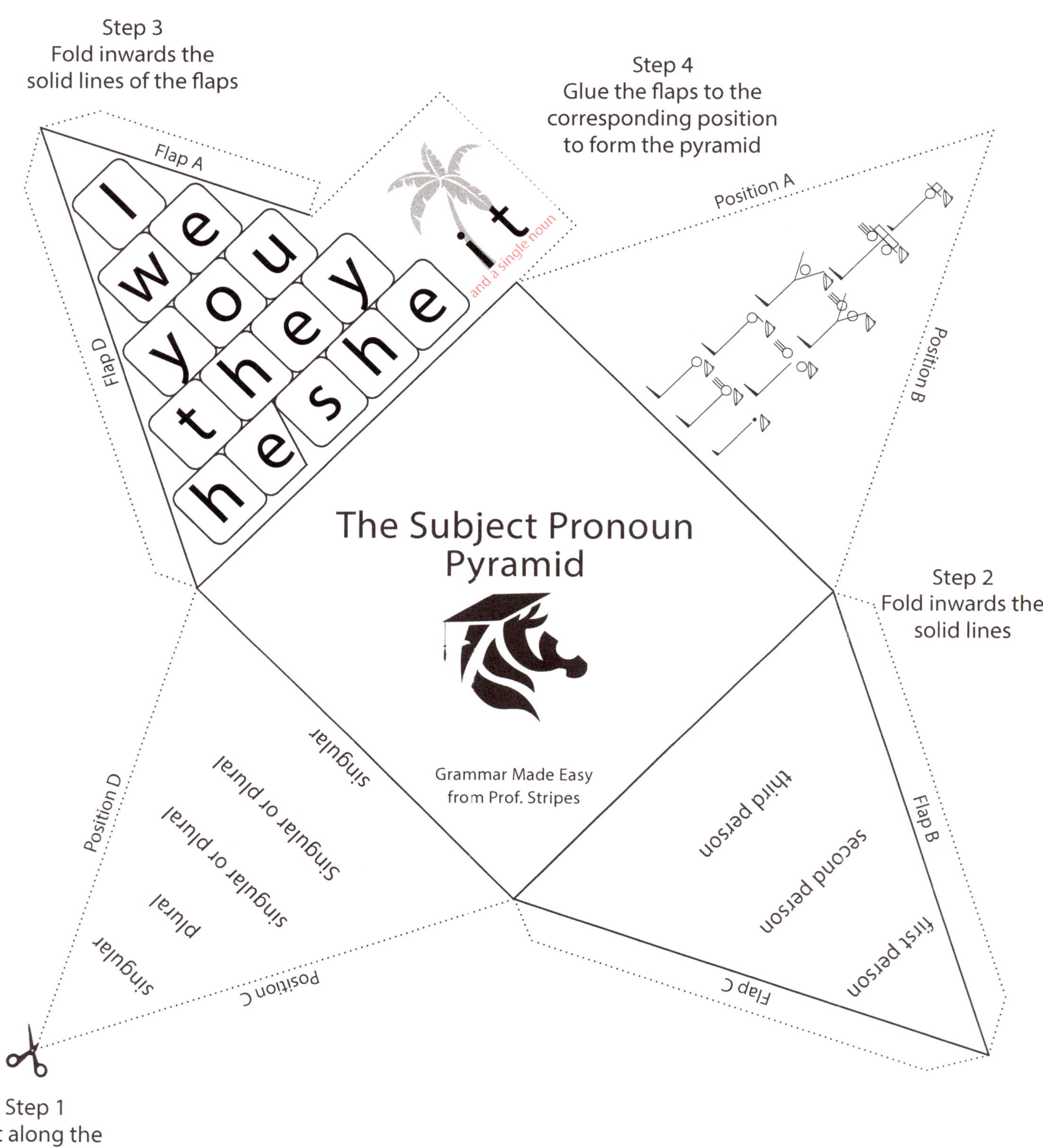

APPENDICES

T he additional supportive information.

> " Get more of the story. "

The Verb Family Tree

There are 3 time zones created from the infinitive of the verb. These are the (simple) tenses: past, present, and future .

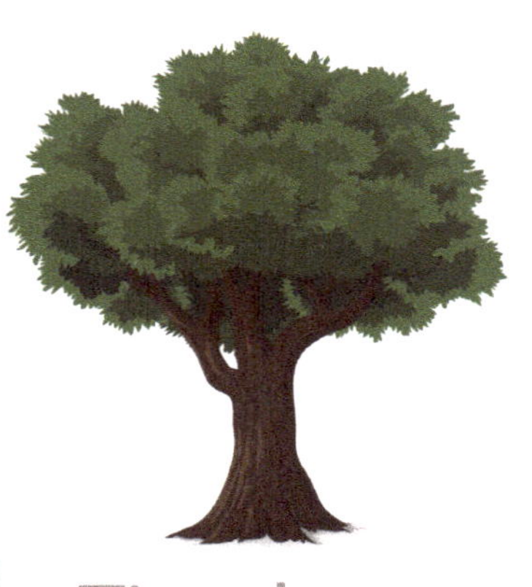

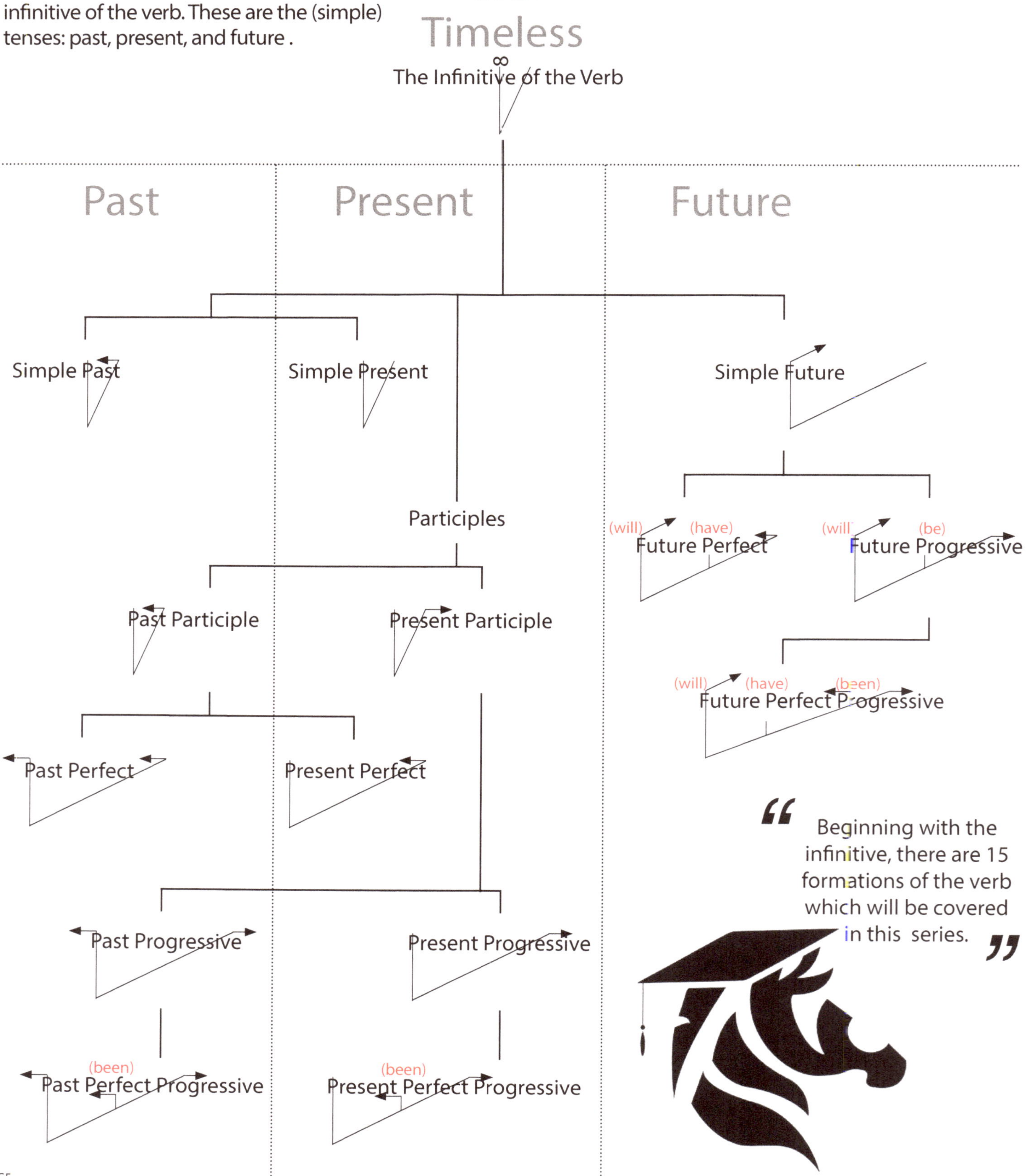

Timeless
∞
The Infinitive of the Verb
Past
Present
Future
Simple Past
Simple Present
Simple Future
Participles
(will) (have)
Future Perfect
(will) (be)
Future Progressive
Past Participle
Present Participle
(will) (have) (been)
Future Perfect Progressive
Past Perfect
Present Perfect
Past Progressive
Present Progressive
(been)
Past Perfect Progressive
(been)
Present Perfect Progressive

“Beginning with the infinitive, there are 15 formations of the verb which will be covered in this series.”

Tenses

The verb is a time traveller: it has the hands of time and they can be pointing, or not pointing, to the past, present, or future.

(Simple) Past Tense

It has already happened. It is history. It was yesterday.

(Simple) Present Tense

This is live! It's happening now! It's today's present!

(Simple) Future Tense

It could happen… in a minute, next day, next year. It's tomorrow's future.

The (Subject) Pronoun Pyramid

The form of the verb needs to match with the main charactor (or subject) of the sentence. There is a pattern in this matching which can be seen using the pronoun pyramid.

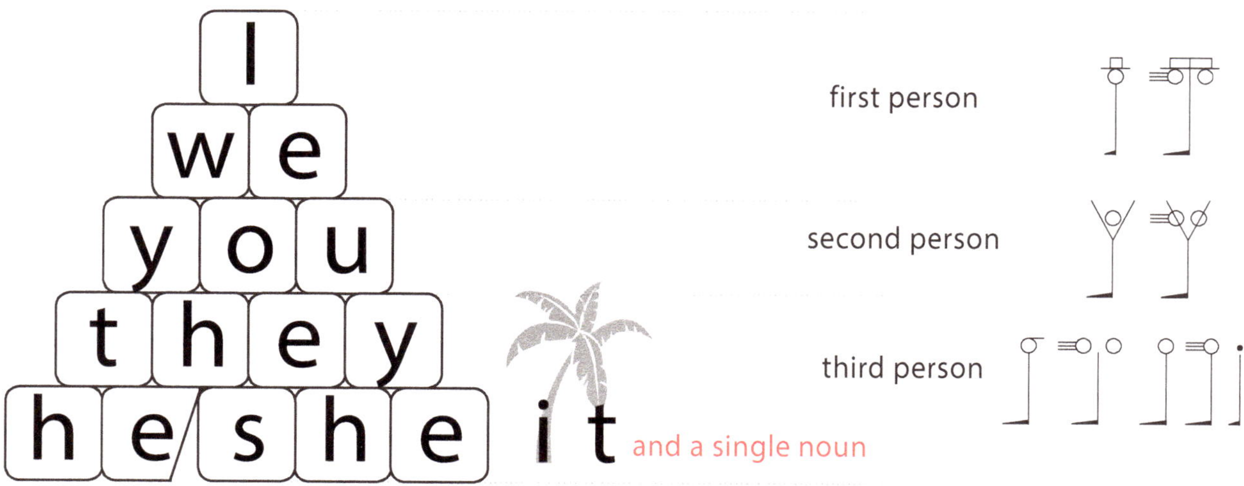

The subject pronoun pyramid: walk, look, help, and call.

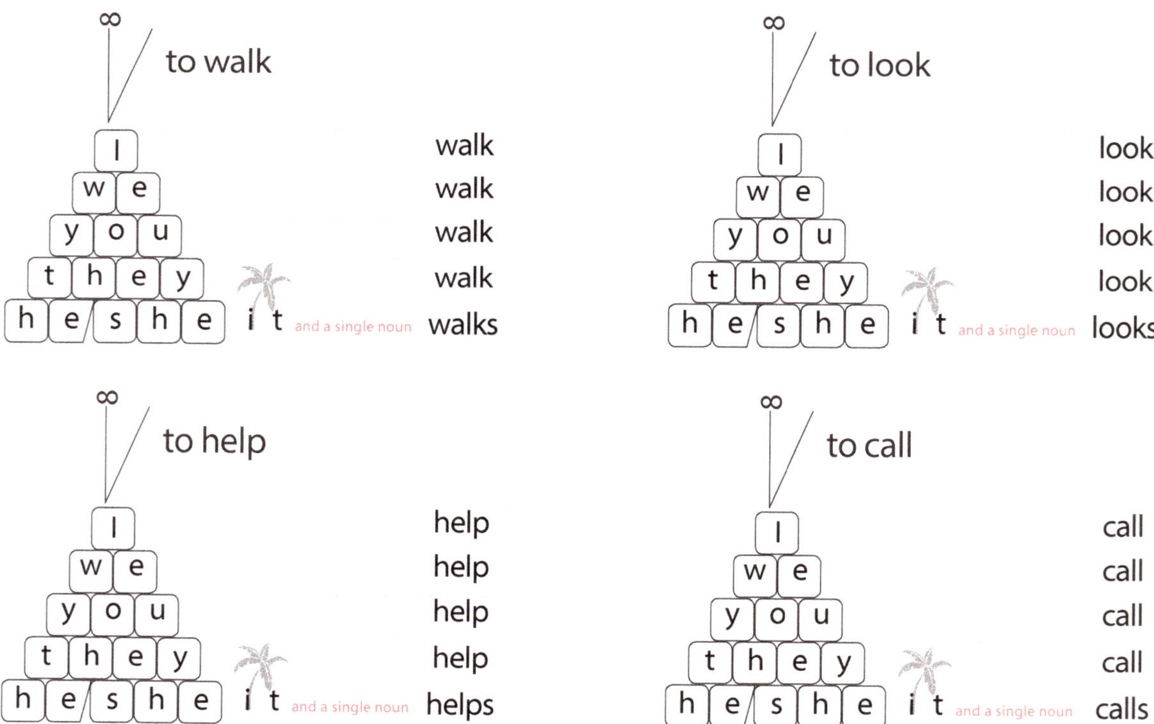

The third person singular is always formed with an "s" suffix. Some irregular verbs which are more complex will be covered later in the book.

"They" Non-binary or Non-Gendered

In English, non-human nouns such as table, chair, car, and others, do not have a gender assigned to them. In these situations, we can use "they" as the non-binary or non-gendered pronoun, especially when we personify the noun (i.e. give a personal nature or human characteristic to something that is non-human).

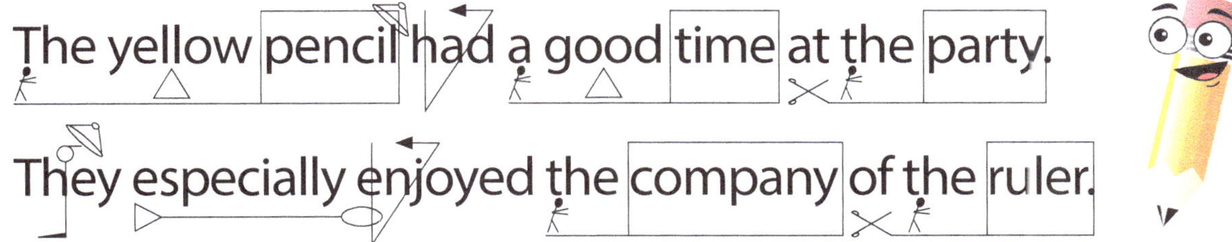

In the above example we can use "they" as the singular subject pronoun of the pencil because the pencil is non-binary and it is non-gendered. We have also learnt about it in the first sentence and it is the main character in the second sentence, so it gets the spotlight.

The Picture therefore for "they" is represented in two ways

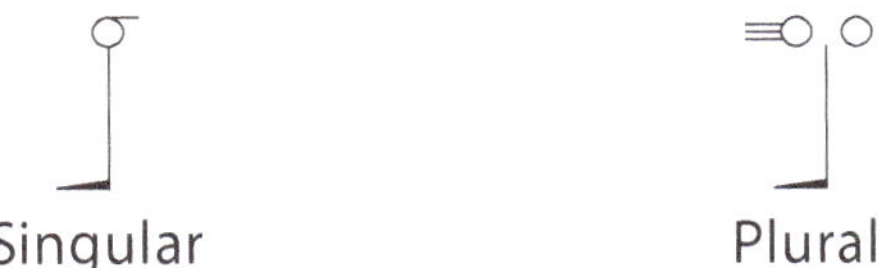

Non-binary or Non-Gendered in Humans

In situations where the person identifies as non-binary, non-gendered, or we do not know, we can use "they" as the singular subject pronoun.

List of Regular Verbs

Some of the regular verbs with their past participle and simple past

to accept (infinitive of the verb) — accepted (simple past) — accepted (past participle)

to borrow — borrowed — borrowed

to call — called — called

to cheer — cheered — cheered

to dance — danced — danced

to enjoy — enjoyed — enjoyed

to fry — fried — fried

to gather — gathered — gathered

to hope — hoped — hoped

List of Regular Verbs (Cont.)

Some of the regular verbs with their past participle and simple past

to introduce	introduced	introduced
(infinitive of the verb)	(simple past)	(past participle)
to jump	jumped	jumped
to kick	kicked	kicked
to laugh	laughed	laughed
to listen	listened	listened
to move	moved	moved
to need	needed	needed
to offer	offered	offered
to play	played	played

List of Regular Verbs (Cont.)

Some of the regular verbs with their past participle and simple past

to purchase	purchased	purchased
(infinitive of the verb)	(simple past)	(past participle)
to question	questioned	questioned
to relax	relaxed	relaxed
to start	started	started
to talk	talked	talked
to use	used	used
to visit	visited	visited
to walk	walked	walked
to yell	yelled	yelled

List of Irregular Verbs

Some of the irregular verbs with their past participle and simple past

to become
(infinitive of the verb)

became
(simple past)

become
(past participle)

to begin

began

begun

to bite

bit

bitten

to build

built

built

to catch

caught

caught

to come

came

come

to do

did

done

to drive

drove

driven

to eat

ate

eaten

List of Irregular Verbs (Cont.)

Some of the irregular verbs with their past participle and simple past

to fall (infinitive of the verb)	fell (simple past)	fallen (past participle)
to feel	felt	felt
to find	found	found
to fly	flew	flown
to give	gave	given
to have	had	had
to hide	hid	hidden
to hold	held	held
to keep	kept	kept

List of Irregular Verbs (Cont.)

Some of the irregular verbs with their past participle and simple past

to know (infinitive of the verb) — knew (simple past) — known (past participle)

to learn — learnt — learnt

to leave — left — left

to make — made — made

to pay — paid — paid

to put — put — put

to read — read — read

to ring — rang — rung

to run — ran — run

List of Irregular Verbs (Cont.)

Some of the irregular verbs with their past participle and simple past

to say (infinitive of the verb) — said (simple past) — said (past participle)

to sleep — slept — slept

to swim — swam — swum

to take — took — taken

to teach — taught — taught

to think — thought — thought

to understand — understood — understood

to wear — wore — worn

to write — wrote — written

Form Class Words

Nouns, adjectives, verbs and adverbs are form class words because they are formed with identifying tags (or suffixes).

"Words are either "Form Class Words" or "Structure Class Words""

Form Class Words Examples

The inifivitive of the verb is tagged by particular suffixes to form other types of words. For example adverbs are formed by tagging adjectives with ly. Forming a noun from a verb is called nominalisation.

adverb	adjective	nominalisation	infinitive of the verb
playfully	playful	player	to play
differently	different	difference	to differ
rebelliously	rebellious	rebellion	to rebel
foolishly	foolish	foolishness	to fool
financially	financial	financier	to finance
hesitantly	hesitant	hesitancy	to hesitate
deceptively	deceptive	deception	to deceive
reasonably	reasonable	reason	to reason
uselessly	useless	use	to use

Form Class Words Exercises

The exercises are grouped in sentences that feature a particular word used in its various forms. These Form Class Words can take different forms from noun, determiner (as a possessive), adjective, verb and adverb. Notice how the form changes with the different tags (suffixes). Remember the most important point is not the spelling, but how the word is used in the sentence. Draw all the Pictures.

Group 1 - The Form Class Word is: ....

The giant lives in his castle.

The giant's castle was gigantic.

He lived in his gigantic castle and ate gigantically big meals.

Eating gigantically the giant needed a giant-sized dishwasher.

Group 2 - The Form Class Word is: ....

Sally was a sensation at the concert.

The concert was sensational.

At her sensational concert she played sensationally.

The media sensationalised Sally's concert.

Group 3 - The Form Class Word is: ....

Dad had a hunger for stew.

The dog was hungry and hungered after the same stew.

Dad's hungry dog sniffed hungrily at the deliciously hot stew.

Form Class Words Answers

The exercises are grouped in sentences that feature a particular word used in its various forms. These Form Class Words can take different forms from noun, determiner (as a possessive), adjective, verb and adverb. Notice how the form changes with the different tags (suffixes). Remember the most important point is not the spelling, but how the word is used in the sentence. Draw all the Pictures.

Group 1 - The Form Class Word is Giant

The giant lives in his castle.

The giant's castle was gigantic.

He lived in his gigantic castle and ate gigantically big meals.

Eating gigantically the giant needed a giant-sized dishwasher.

Group 2 - The Form Class Word is Sensation

Sally was a sensation at the concert.

The concert was sensational.

At her sensational concert she played sensationally.

The media sensationalised Sally's concert.

Group 3 - The Form Class Word is Hungry

Dad had a hunger for stew.

The dog was hungry and hungered after the same stew.

Dad's hungry dog sniffed hungrily at the deliciously hot stew.

Structure Class Words

S tructure class words are words that signal how the form class words relate to each other in a sentence. There are far fewer structure class words than form class words.

> "
> Words are either
> "Form Class Words" or
> "Structure Class Words"
> "

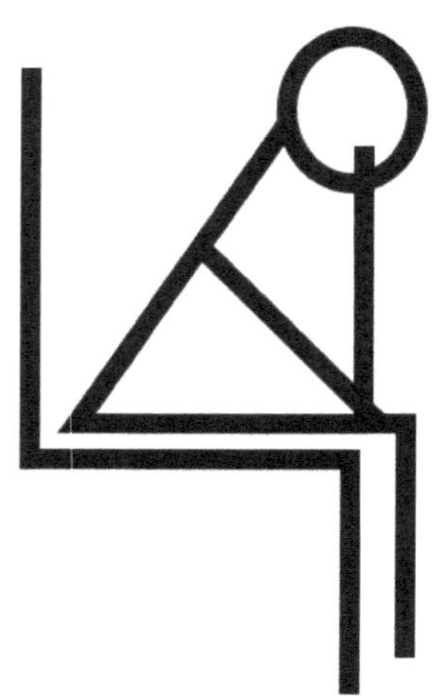

Structure Class Words

Structure class words help determine the function of the sentence. They do not have variations in their form like Form class words.

Determiners and prepositionas are structure class words: they can't be formed; they give structure to the sentence.

Structure class words have not really changed since Shakespeare's time: they've been around for 400 years.

More On Structure Class Words

Structure class words can be determiners, auxiliaries, adverbs, prepositions, conjunctions, relative pronouns and pronouns.

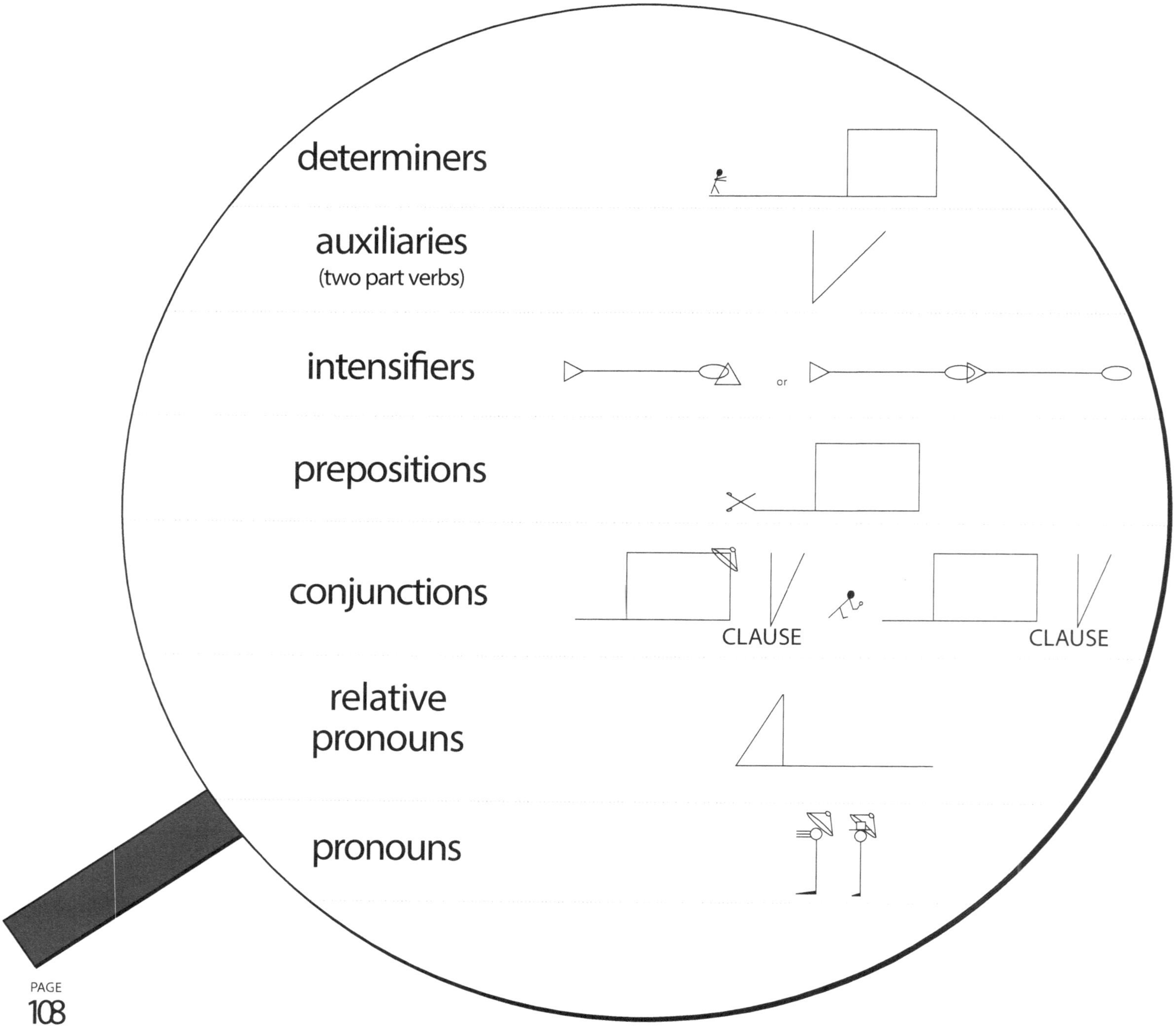

determiners

auxiliaries
(two part verbs)

intensifiers

prepositions

conjunctions

relative
pronouns

pronouns

Glossary

> **Pictorial Grammar Theory is a useful tool for learning English grammar**

 # Glossary of Pictures

Book 1- Beginner

Picture Number	Picture	Description
1		Noun
2		Spotlight
3		The Shadow On The Noun
4		The Determiner
5		The Adjective
6		The Preposition
7		The Verb
8a		The Adverb with Adjectives
8b		The Adverb with Verbs
9		The Conjunction
10		The Relative Pronoun & It's Clause

Glossary of Pictures

Book 2 - Intermediate

Picture Number	Picture	Description
11		Subject Pronoun "I"
12		Subject Pronoun "We"
13		Subject Pronoun "You" (singular form)
14		Subject Pronoun "You" (plural form)
15		Subject Pronoun "He"
16		Subject Pronoun "She"
17		Subject Pronoun "It"
18		Subject Pronoun "They" (singular) and (plural) form
19a		The Infinitive of the Verb
19b		The Infinitive Phrase
19c		The Present & Past Participle of the Verb

 Glossary of Pictures

Book 2 - Intermediate (Cont.)

Picture Number	Picture	Description
19d	past present	The Present & Past Participle Phrase
19e		The Present Tense of the Verb
20	See Page 58 or 93	The (Subject) Pronoun Pyramid
19f		The Past Tense of the Verb

The Pictorial Grammar Theory Series

Book 1: Beginner

Book 2: Intermediate

Book 3: Professional

Book 4: Expert

Book 5: Master

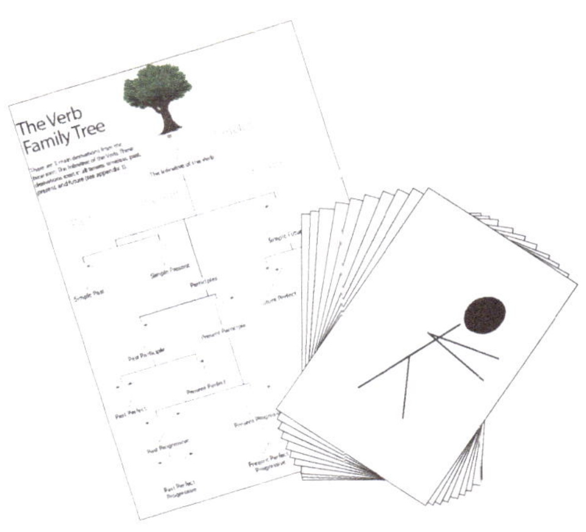

And additional resources at

www.profstripes.com